The Welfare State

a general theory

Paul Spicker

SAGE Publications

London • Thousand Oaks • New Delhi

First published 2000

 SAGE Publications Ltd
6 Bonhill Street
London EC2A 4PU

SAGE Publications Inc
2455 Teller Road
Thousand Oaks, California 91320

SAGE Publications India Pvt Ltd
32, M-Block Market
Greater Kailash – I
New Delhi 110 048

British Library Cataloguing in Publication data

A catalogue record for this book is available
from the British Library

ISBN 0 7619 6704 4
ISBN 0 7619 6705 2 (pbk)

Library of Congress catalog card record available

Typeset by Mayhew Typesetting, Rhayader, Powys
Printed and bound in Great Britain by Athenaeum Press, Gateshead

CONTENTS

METHOD

This book is a study in social policy, an academic subject concerned with the application of the social sciences to the study of social welfare. Social policy does not have a distinctive disciplinary approach. The material which is used in this study is drawn from a number of sources, principally sociology, philosophy, politics and economics; at other times, there are references to material from history, psychology, anthropology and law.

The argument develops a general theory of the welfare state. What is meant by a 'welfare state' will be explained in the course of the argument, but it is also important to explain what a 'general theory' is, and so what kind of book this is.

Theory in social science

Theory in social science begins with the process of describing empirical material, by disentangling facts from each other and laying out a framework through which it can subsequently be analysed and understood. Scientific knowledge generally needs much more than description to flourish, but description comes first: biology has its taxonomies, carefully describing the classes of species, and social science has its descriptive systems, which help to explain what is happening and why it matters. The best-known schemes for describing welfare states are probably those introduced by Richard Titmuss[1] and Gøsta Esping-Andersen.[2] These models have important deficiencies,[3] and the kinds of generalization

---

1 R. Titmuss (1974) *Social policy: an introduction*, London: Allen and Unwin.

2 G. Esping-Andersen (1990) *The three worlds of welfare capitalism*, Cambridge: Polity.

3 P. Spicker (1996) 'Normative comparisons of social security systems', in L. Hantrais and S. Mangen (eds) *Cross-national research methods in the social sciences*, London: Pinter, pp. 66–75.

they make are difficult to relate to welfare states in practice.[4] This book is concerned with a different type of description, and it takes a different approach.

The method of the book depends on a closely structured, and sometimes formal, reasoning. Formal reasoning in social science has largely been confined to economic theory, though there is also a specialized literature within sociology.[5] Economic analysis, and particularly welfare economics, is largely based in a formalistic argument which describes the implications of certain types of action, rather than the question of whether people really behave in that way. If certain conditions obtain, the argument runs, then, other things being equal, certain consequences will follow. This kind of reasoning has been applied at several points in the argument of this book. For example, comparative advantage – the idea that people can produce more through specialization and exchange than they can individually – is not a hypothesis; it can be demonstrated arithmetically or geometrically.[6] The proof, which is given later in this book, is not falsifiable, any more than the statement that '2 + 2 = 4' is falsifiable. References to the evidence serve, not to prove or disprove the theory, but to ground it – to show whether such conditions do, in fact, apply. This is the pattern of much of the argument of the book. The method is strongly associated with analytical theory, but this book is not simply an exercise in abstract reasoning. The formal arguments are related to the available evidence. This is not an argument *a priori*; it is grounded theory.

Grounded theory is not the same thing as scientific deduction. Part of the received wisdom of social science is that a scientific theory should be empirically testable, and so that it must be falsifiable.[7] This is right, but it is only half right. In natural science there is a place for classificatory systems, and for formal reasoning. (Karl Popper, the principal exponent of the test of falsifiability, accepted that it did not apply to every form of scientific activity.)[8] The same applies to social science. Blaug, writing about economic theory, points to the difficulty of distinguishing testable propositions from abstract principles which correspond to practice, and the problem of proof when so much of social science is based in probabilities rather than certainties. He argues:

---

4 D. Mabbett and H. Bolderson (1999) 'Theories and methods in comparative social policy', in J. Clasen (ed.) *Comparative social policy: concepts, theories and methods*, Oxford: Blackwell.

5 R. Boudon (1974) *The logic of sociological explanations*, Harmondsworth: Penguin Education.

6 See e.g. M. Parkin, M. Powell and K. Matthews (1997) *Economics*, 3rd edition, Harlow: Addison-Wesley, pp. 55–59.

7 K. Popper (1968) *The logic of scientific discovery*, London: Hutchinson.

8 Popper, interviewed in J. Horgan (1996) *The end of science*, Boston: Little, Brown, pp. 38–39.

A 'theory' is not to be condemned merely because it is as yet untestable, nor even if it is so framed as to preclude testing, provided it draws attention to a significant problem and provides a framework for its discussion from which a testable implication may some day emerge.[9]

Dahrendorf, from the perspective of sociology, proposes a test: that there has to be at least some puzzle, a 'riddle of experience', which needs to be solved.[10] This book addresses several riddles of this kind. The questions which it is trying to answer are: What is a welfare state? Why have welfare states developed? What can they be expected to do?

There is plenty of evidence available about welfare states; the problem is to interpret it. There is a wide range of historical interpretations of the development of the welfare states. For present purposes, they can largely be represented in terms of two very different, competing approaches. One set of historical explanations locates welfare primarily in the development of public provision, the dominance of legal measures and political decisions, citizenship and the growth of state responsibility.[11] Another sees the state as only a part of much more broadly based social processes: the development of welfare is described in terms of collective action, the extension of mutualism and the growth of solidarity.[12] The dominant theoretical models of the welfare state have drawn mainly on the first branch; they begin with the state. This book, by contrast, begins with society; the state does not appear until the third part. Unlike many socially based accounts,[13] the stress in the analysis of relationships falls on social relationships and responsibilities, rather than the logic of industrialism or the development of labour movements. The welfare

---

9 M. Blaug (1968) *Economic theory in retrospect*, London: Heinemann, p. 673.

10 R. Dahrendorf (1968) 'Out of utopia: toward a reorientation of sociological analysis', in L. Coser and B. Rosenberg (eds) *Sociological theory*, New York: Macmillan, 1976.

11 E.g. M. Bruce (1968) *The coming of the welfare state*, London: Batsford; D. Fraser (1973) *The evolution of the British welfare state*, London: Macmillan; W. Trattner (1984) *From Poor Law to welfare state*, New York: Free Press; P. Flora and A. Heidenheimer (1981) *The welfare state in comparative perspective*, New York: Basic Books; D. Ashford (1986) *The emergence of the welfare states*, Oxford: Blackwell.

12 P. Baldwin (1990) *The politics of social solidarity*, Cambridge: Cambridge University Press; H.E. Raynes (1960) *Social security in Britain*, London: Pitman; D. Green (1993) *Reinventing civil society*, London: Institute for Economic Affairs; F. Chatagner (1993) *La Protection sociale*, Paris: Le Monde Editions, ch. 1; J-J. Dupeyroux (1998) *Droit de la sécurité sociale*, Paris: Dalloz.

13 E.g. G. Rimlinger (1971) *Welfare policy and industrialisation in Europe, America and Russia*, New York: John Wiley; J. Saville (1975) 'The welfare state: an historical approach', in E. Butterworth and R. Holman (eds) *Social welfare in modern Britain*, Glasgow: Fontana.

state is placed in a social context, and the book maps it in relation to its different elements.

In the study of social policy, theory has a further purpose, which is the analysis of normative elements. Normative theory is sometimes seen as idealistic; David Hume established the central principle that it is not possible to go from the way things ought to be to understand the way they are.[14] Social science differs here from moral philosophy, because – as Hume himself recognized[15] – the social construction of norms, what people believe to be right, depends on what actually happens. The study of these issues in social policy is not, and cannot be, value-neutral. It is possible to examine policies in a neutral fashion, seeing whether they achieve their stated ends, but the study of social policy has to consider whether the ends are appropriate as well as whether they are achieved. This offers a basis for evaluation, and criteria by which the welfare state can be assessed.

A general theory

A general theory is not a theory of everything. The theory in this book is general in the sense that it is intended to offer insights which are generally applicable. The focus falls principally on economically developed countries, because that is where the welfare states have mainly arisen, though, as explained in the course of the text, the arguments are not strictly confined to developed countries. It is not possible to argue that the argument extends to every form of society, but the book is not about Britain, or the US, or the European Union, or South East Asia, or any other particular welfare state.

The welfare states are diverse and complex, and attention has mainly been focused on the differences between them, rather than their similarities. Gøsta Esping-Andersen's classification of welfare state regimes is based on an analysis of variations. Researchers who have tried to apply Esping-Andersen's research closely to practice have found it is almost impossible to tie in the specifics with the broad models.[16] 'The devil is in the detail', Ditch comments. The root of the problem is that Esping-Andersen is concerned with variation – the things that make welfare states different – and there are more grounds for variation than he can encompass sensibly in a limited typology.

---

14 D. Hume (1751) *An enquiry concerning the principles of morals*, Oxford: Oxford University Press, 1998.

15 D. Hume (1748) *Of the original contract*, in E. Barker (ed.) *Social contract*, Oxford: Oxford University Press, 1971.

16 D. Mabbett and H. Bolderson, 'Theories and methods', and J. Ditch 'Full circle: a second coming for social assistance?' both in J. Clasen (ed.) *Comparative social policy*, Oxford: Blackwell (1999).

Political and historical accounts of welfare tend to emphasize the disparate, idiosyncratic character of welfare systems. Social explanations – which, Baldwin notes, have taken a beating in recent years[17] – point to common issues and pressures. It is quite possible to argue on the evidence that welfare states have nothing in common; they may have a family resemblance but the variation between them is so great that no generalization can be made. That position is tenable across a wide range of activity of welfare states, and for many areas of social policy it is so obviously true that it is difficult to argue against it. This leaves us, however, a central puzzle, because welfare states do still have something in common: they are characterized by collective action for social protection. It is not the differences between welfare states which present a problem to be explained; it is the similarities. (To that extent, this book shares its agenda with de Swaan's historical overview, *In the care of the state*.[18] However, its approach, and its argument, are very different.) A theory which can explain these similarities has to be general.

At this level, the theory cannot be concerned with many specific problems (like, say, mechanisms for delivering benefits, or for user involvement) which an analysis of welfare might reasonably refer to. More fundamentally, some important issues – like labour movements, gender, or political bargaining – receive limited emphasis, because they help to explain variations in welfare states, rather than common factors. Because the argument of the book excludes specific points and issues, it describes only a small part of the whole. But that part provides an explanation of the relationships between a range of disparate issues, and a framework within which other issues can be considered.

The general theory in this book is one of several. Marxism, functionalism and feminism, amongst other schools of thought, have offered general arguments applied across a range of welfare states.[19] Conventionally, arguments are tested by being subjected to opposing points of view, and there is often an advantage in anticipating criticism; certainly some readers will pre-judge the argument, on the basis of views they have long held. However, this book does not review different schools of thought. The views of neo-liberals or Marxists depend on an elaborately developed understanding of society, and I have not considered them in any depth here; I have referred to them when they are relevant. Although the process of criticizing such work has been important in the development of my own thinking, the argument of the book has not been

17 Baldwin (1990) p. 288.

18 A. de Swaan (1988) *In the care of the state*, Cambridge: Polity.

19 See e.g. R. Mishra (1981) *Society and social policy*, Basingstoke: Macmillan; V. George and P. Wilding (1994) *Welfare and ideology*, Hemel Hempstead: Harvester Wheatsheaf; M. Mullard and P. Spicker (1998) *Social policy in a changing society*, London: Routledge.

constructed from the ruins of other theories. It begins from a completely
different set of premises from most other books about welfare; there is no
obvious way to go from there to here. For the most part the book makes
its own case, in its own way.

The structure of the book

The book consists of a set of hierarchically ordered propositions. The
argument is built on three basic propositions. They are not self-evident;
each is discussed and explained in the course of the argument.

I   *People live in society, and have obligations to each other.*
II   *Welfare is obtained and maintained through social action.*
III *The welfare state is a means of promoting and maintaining welfare in*
     society.

Each of these statements is developed through a series of sub-
propositions.

I   *People live in society, and have obligations to each other.*
     I.1   People live in society.
     I.2   Social relationships are patterned and structured.
     I.3   Within social networks, people have obligations to help each
            other.
     I.4   People and communities have to act morally.

II   *Welfare is obtained and maintained through social action.*
     II.1   People have needs, which require a social response.
     II.2   People have economic and social rights.
     II.3   Social protection is necessary to secure welfare.
     II.4   Welfare implies redistribution.

III *The welfare state is a means of promoting and maintaining welfare in*
     society.
     III.1 'Government is a contrivance of human wisdom to provide for
            human wants.'
     III.2 The welfare states provide social protection.
     III.3 Welfare is promoted and maintained through social policy.
     III.4 The welfare states have a wide range of options through which
            social policies can be pursued, but they can be assessed by
            common criteria.

These second-level propositions are explored in a further series of propositions, and the third level is considered in turn at a fourth level. They
are not substantively different kinds of statements – the 'levels' or tiers

simply reflect the structure of the argument. The propositions are num-
bered according to their position in the hierarchy, so that:

I   is a first-level proposition;
I.1   is second level;
I.1.a   is third level;
I.1.a.i   is fourth level; and
I.1.a.i(1) is fifth level.

The full set of propositions is listed in a summary at the end of the book.

I PEOPLE AND SOCIETY

I People live in society, and have
   obligations to each other.

THE PERSON

I.1 People live in society

People in society
I.1.a	*People live with other people.*
I.1.a.i	People in society are interdependent.
I.1.a.ii	Social interaction follows common patterns.

The nature of the personal
I.1.b	*People are defined by their social relationships.*
I.1.b.i	The personal is the social.
	I.1.b.i.(1) Personal differences are largely not explicable in terms of biology.
I.1.b.ii	The 'individual' is a myth.

Social obligations
I.1.c	*Social relationships generate obligations between people.*
I.1.c.i	Interdependence implies reciprocity.
I.1.c.ii	Each person must have regard to others.
	I.1.c.ii(1) If I am not for myself, who will be for me?
	I.1.c.ii(2) If I am only for myself, what am I?
	I.1.c.ii(3) If not now, when?
I.1.c.iii	Obligations have to be counterbalanced with rights.

People in society

I.1.a People live with other people.

A social life is life with other people, and for the vast majority of us, it is the only life we will ever know or ever have. Most of us 'live with other people' for a large part of our lives: typically, this means that we live in families or households, and for most of us the family is basic to social integration, particularly in childhood. There are, of course, many other arrangements, in which people share accommodation and basic facilities with people beyond a family or household; people may also live in schools, group homes, institutions, religious orders, military bases or communes.

When people live alone, they do not generally live in isolation from other people. 'Living alone' means simply that people do not have immediate contact with others in the household where they live. Many of us do live alone at some time in our lives, and there are societies in which the numbers of people living alone are increasing. However, this generally occurs long after they have been introduced to the patterns of life, expectations and norms which are part of life in any society.

I.1.a.i   *People in society are interdependent.*

Society involves much more than proximity. Beyond the immediate circle of family and intimates, contact leads to interaction, and inter-action leads to exchange – the exchange of goods, of symbols, of possessions, even of relatives.[20] People become interdependent. Society is formed from a complex series of social relationships, and inter-dependence is fundamental to those relationships.

Interdependence means that people's lives are conditioned by the lives of other people. This is most obvious in interpersonal relationships, but it is no less true of material affairs, and the minutiae of everyday life. Interdependence is so much a part of our lives that it can be difficult to recognize; people can only see a small part at any one time. In material terms, interdependence shapes everything we use or possess – the food we eat, the clothes we wear, the places we live in. The products of exchange dominate the physical environment, including roads and buildings, fields and the countryside. In developed countries, self-sufficiency is so rare as to be almost inconceivable. People may build their own houses, or grow their own meals, but in general they do not do it with tools and materials they prepare themselves.

Some writers have seen exchange as the fundamental cement which holds a society together;[21] it means not just that strangers can interact in ways which are mutually beneficial, but that codes are held in common to make it possible for them to do so. Interdependence means more than economic exchange; it leads to shared norms, expectations and patterns

---

20 C. Lévi-Strauss (1969) *The elementary structures of kinship*, London: Eyre and Spottiswoode.

21 E.g. M. Mauss (1925) *The gift: forms and functions of exchange in archaic societies*, London: Cohen and West, 1966; G.C. Homans (1961) *Social behaviour*, London: Routledge and Kegan Paul; P. Ekeh (1974) *Social exchange theory*, London: Heinemann.

of behaviour. We have relationships with many people. Even when the relationships are remote, we usually have some idea of how to react to others. People share codes of behaviour, and expectations about the way in which others will behave.

I.1.a.ii *Social interaction follows common patterns.*

The relationships which people form do not occur randomly. The process of contact and interaction is complex, and that can give the impression of randomness and chance. For example, people may seem to fall in love randomly, but the truth is that most people meet their partners in predictable locations – home, work, formal social events or in an extended circle of friends. Love is principally a matter of geography, though it is moderated by cultural influences.[22] Consciously or unconsciously, people take into account social expectations; because so many codes are shared, information about a person's background and approach is rapidly absorbed from personal presentation, dress, appearance and demeanour.

People occupy roles in society, and these roles structure their social relationships.[23] A role is a part that someone plays; the part defines the kinds of things the person does. This is most obviously the case with occupational roles; social introductions often begin with the question, 'What do you do?', and the familiar answers – police officer, pharmacist, refuse disposal operative, circus acrobat – conjure a picture, not just of the job, but of the person's patterns of life, education and social milieu. Equally, there are other kinds of role – as parents, patients, even bystanders – which mean that people who find themselves in a situation or a relationship have some idea of how to behave, and what to expect. The role defines, not just what people do, but what they can be expected to do.

People tend to occupy, not one role, but many. No one is just a teacher, only a daughter, nothing but an old person – or, if they were, we would think there is something seriously wrong with their life. But when we know that someone is a professional artist, mother of four, postgraduate student and member of a feminist reading group, we begin to get a picture of the person. (In this case it is a caricature, because there is not enough information here to show the whole picture, but at least it is a start.) To the sociologist, Dahrendorf once wrote, people are defined by their roles.[24] The roles summarize the range of relationships that a person has; the

---

22 R. Baron and D. Byrne (1994) *Social psychology: understanding human interaction*, 7th edition, Boston: Allyn and Bacon, ch. 7.

23 M. Banton (1965) *Roles*, London: Tavistock; T. Sarbin and V. Allen (1968) 'Role theory', in G. Lindzey and E. Aronson (eds) *Handbook of social psychology*, I, Reading, MA: Addison-Wesley.

24 R. Dahrendorf (1973) *Homo sociologicus*, London: Routledge and Kegan Paul.

relationships cover the circumstances in which the person reacts with other people.

The nature of the personal

I.1.b People are defined by their social relationships.

In sociology, a person is defined by his or her social relationships – that is, relationships to other people. This view may seem strange, because many of us would make the assumption that a person is the same thing as a human being. There can be, however, persons who are not human beings. A corporation, a firm or a trust can be a person in law. Companies can own and dispose of property, they can be insulted, and they can take action.

The converse of this position is that it may be possible to be human without being recognized as a person. A person whose social relationships cease, and whose property is dissolved and distributed, may continue to exist in body but not in other respects. People are socially dead if they are left without any social roles; they become non-persons. This may be the position, unfortunately, of people in long-stay institutions.[25] 'Social death' does not imply that a person vanishes altogether, because in social terms people who are physically dead do not really cease to exist, either. They have been part of a pattern of social relationships, and aspects of those relationships continue to apply after death. People can leave wills, which determine the use of their property after their death. Courts in England can require a dead person's estate to continue to support people who were supported when the dead person was alive.[26] Death is not the end, then, though it has to be admitted it is something of an inconvenience.

This view of personhood has been criticized as 'oversocialized',[27] because there is more to people than their social identity. There are certainly aspects of human conduct which are not conditioned by society, but they are not for the most part those aspects which we value. Those aspects of our lives which are most directly animal are seen through the glass of social relationships; we learn to eat, to walk, and to sleep in the patterns which are expected in our society. (Sometimes, of course, these issues come into conflict; many human problems, like illness, insomnia or incontinence, become vastly complex because of their

25 E. Miller and G. Gwynne (1972) *A life apart*, London: Tavistock, p. 80.

26 The law is in the Inheritance (Family Provision) Act 1938, the Intestates Act 1952, and the Family Provision Act 1966.

27 D. Wrong (1967) 'The oversocialised conception of man in modern sociology', in H.J. Demerath and R. Peterson (eds) *System change and conflict*, New York: Free Press.

social implications.) Love, honour, justice, honesty and wisdom are social in their nature. Qualities like diligence, skill and creativity may be admired, but whether they are valued depends on what they are applied to. It is only in a social context that people can do the things in life which are worthwhile.

I.1.b.i *The personal is the social.*

Social relationships are fundamental to our humanity. People tend to think of their thoughts and feelings as personal, and individual to themselves: each human being has distinct thoughts, feelings and memories, which are private and unique to that being. Gilbert Ryle, the philosopher, argued that because language and reactions are formed socially, in interactions with other people, our thoughts, feelings and memories can never truly be 'private'. We learn about them in the same way as other people do; we observe our actions, see how we feel, and record the information.[28] This also means, of course, that our ability to understand ourselves depends on our ability to understand other people. Introspection is not the way to enlightenment.

The language we use, the way we use our senses, the way we relate to other people, the terms on which we interact, are social in nature; they are shaped by the society in which we live. Children are not found under gooseberry bushes, with all their faculties fully formed; they are born into families and communities, and over time they are socialized, absorbing the codes, patterns of thought and ways of life which shape their world and the people around them. From the extraordinary case of the Wild Boy of Aveyron, we have a vague, if disputed, idea of what a human being might be like without this kind of contact; raised without language and social contact, the Wild Boy learned to speak and to live with others, but not to reason abstractly.[29] Similar conditions have been found in some children who have been severely neglected and isolated from others.

I.1.b.i.(1) Personal differences are largely not explicable in terms of biology.

The strongest arguments against a social view of people are based in biology. Collectively, the role played by human biology is evident: people are born, they develop physically, they have physical needs. If they are able to reproduce, they can only do so for part of the life-cycle. They grow old, they die. Gender, age, reproduction and health are vitally

---

28 G. Ryle (1963) *The concept of mind*, Harmondsworth: Penguin.
29 H. Lane (1979) *The wild boy of Aveyron*, St Albans: Granada.

important elements of any society. This is the framework within which human life is set, and much of it is taken for granted in the understanding of social life.

For personal differences to be explained biologically, however, more is needed. There would have to be an association of social behaviour with a person's biological history. An argument which has recurred since the mid-nineteenth century is that human biology, breeding or genetics is central to the patterns of behaviour which people exhibit in society. If this is correct, there should be some association of particular behaviours with certain genes, or at least some degree of continuity in behaviours between generations of a family. This is the Philosopher's Stone of genetic research; after more than a century of trying, neither contention has been supported by evidence. Claims for specific inherited behaviours, like the genetic origins of homosexuality or crime, have not even attempted to identify whether the gene is generally associated with the characteristic.[30] If there are biological predispositions to behaviour, expressed for example in aggression or the response to stress, they are hard to trace; the influence of social circumstances on these factors is profound.[31] As for families, studies of intergenerational continuity of social circumstances have found that any attempt to identify patterns within families is dwarfed by the magnitude of fluctuations created by other factors, such as economic conditions, education or housing.[32]

The strongest argument for a link between individual biology and social circumstances is that some people may have organic conditions, like physical impairments, which lead to differentiation. This is hotly disputed: proponents of a 'social model of disability' have argued that different societies respond to such conditions in very different ways, which makes it impossible to explain social circumstances sensibly in terms of physical differences.[33] This may leave individual biology with some role, but it is a limited one.

I.1.b.ii   The 'individual' is a myth.

Myths are important, because they change the way in which people understand problems. It is a fundamental axiom of sociology that, if people believe something to be true, the belief is true in its social

---

30 S. Jones (1993) *The language of the genes*, London: Flamingo, ch. 12.

31 A. Mummendey (1996) 'Aggressive behaviour', in M. Hewstone, W. Stroebe and G. Stephenson (eds) *Introduction to social psychology*, 2nd edition, Oxford: Blackwell; M. Argyle (1992) *The social psychology of everyday life*, London: Routledge, ch. 10.

32 M. Rutter and C. Madge (1976) *Cycles of disadvantage*, London: Heinemann; M. Brown (ed.) (1983) *The structure of disadvantage*, London: Heinemann.

33 M. Oliver (1996) *Understanding disability*, London: Macmillan, ch. 3.

consequences.[34] The idea of the solitary individual is one of the most
pervasive myths in Western society – Robinson Crusoe, trapped on a
desert island and startled at the sight of another person's footprint. As a
general description of the human condition, the idea is absurd; but as a
myth it exercises a powerful influence over human conduct, on the way
we understand ourselves and our relations with others. The ideology of
'rugged individualism' has been powerful in the politics of the United
States: it appears in the exaltation of the individual, mistrust of government and 'big business', the legend of the frontier, and the cultural fetish
of bearing arms, hunting and woodcraft.

Many analyses of society begin with the 'individual': the independent,
self-determining, isolated adult who makes his or her own way in the
world. This is a fictive construct rather than reality. People do not, and
cannot, live in isolation (► I.1.a). They are interdependent, not independent (► I.1.a.i); they live through society (► I.1.a.ii), not according to
their inner lights, and no decision outside the social context has meaning
(► I.1.b.i). From the argument above, the individual may or may not be a
person, and people are important; but the characteristics which make us
human, and which we value, are social (► I.1.b), and it makes no real
sense to talk of individuals divorced from a social context.

As a description of the way that people live, then, individualism is
false. But individualism is not just a description, or a myth; it is also a
method, and a moral position. As a method, it makes it possible to
consider each element in a social grouping separately, and so to understand the interactions more clearly. As a moral position, individualism
asserts that each human being is valuable, irrespective of social status;
that people have rights; and that no social order can justifiably sacrifice a
human being for the sake of the greater good. These arguments have
played a major part in struggles against oppression, and they are not to
be underestimated. Societies and social orders can work against their
members; they can be oppressive, and they can stifle human development. The individualist approach is a useful safeguard and counter-
balance to this tendency, and in the discussion which follows that is how
it will be applied.

Social obligations

I.1.c   Social relationships generate obligations between people.

Social contact depends on communication, interaction and exchange
(► I.1.a.ii). Relationships develop as these elements are repeated and form

---

34 W. Thomas and F. Znaniecki (1920) *The Polish peasant in Europe and America*,
Chicago: Chicago University Press.

recognizable patterns of contact and interaction. Patterned behaviour generates expectations, and expectations develop into the codes which govern many of our social interactions. Some of these are relatively trivial, and they are liable to be relegated to the field of etiquette; it is not a major offence to eat peas with a knife, or to cut one's toenails in public. However, even trivial expectations – that people will not stare when conversing, or that they will stand at a certain distance – are important for governing behaviour between relative strangers, and they are an essential part of interaction with strangers.[35] Other codes, like those governing exchange or handling money, are much more serious; without them, trade and the exchange of money would become impossible. Because people are born into societies with extended, developed patterns of behaviour, it can be difficult to identify just how or where the process starts, and there are many potential explanations; for the purposes of the argument, however, it is enough to recognize that they are there.

In a social context, such expectations are often accompanied by sanctions. People who do not conform to expectations are censured, rejected, even punished. Expectations acquire, in consequence, the character of obligations. These are referred to as 'norms'. A social norm is a generalized expectation, subject to a sanction. It is generalized because it is widely held. This does not mean that it has to be held by everyone; only that it must be held widely enough to be generally understood. Disseminating and sharing views are possible because ideas, opinions and beliefs are formed through social interaction. The process is not 'subjective', in the sense that it depends on the individual observer, but it is 'intersubjective' – based on the views, values and feelings of a wide range of people in a society.[36]

I.1.c.i Interdependence implies reciprocity.

Some key obligations come into being because of social interdependence. There is a 'norm of reciprocity'.[37] Reciprocity is commonly represented in two very different ways. Balanced (or 'restricted') exchange happens when people exchange goods directly, offering quids for quos. This is the general expectation in trade or contract, and for the most part it is unquestioned. There is also, however, 'generalized' exchange, in which the return which is made may not have to be made by the person who has received the goods. The principle is illustrated in Figure 1: exchange

35 M. Argyle (1967) *The psychology of interpersonal behaviour*, Harmondsworth: Penguin.

36 P. Berger and T. Luckmann (1967) *The social construction of reality*, New York: Anchor.

37 A. Gouldner (1960) 'The norm of reciprocity', *American Sociological Review*, 25 (2): 161–177.

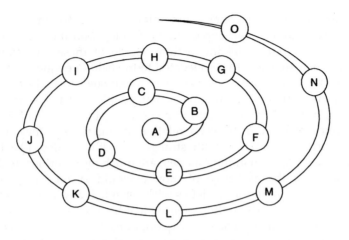

Figure 1   *Generalized reciprocity*

links one person to the next, in an indefinitely large circuit. A gives to B, B to C, C to D, D to E, and so on. The circuit could be completed at any time, but it does not have to be.

The concept of generalized reciprocity emerged from anthropological studies: the work of Malinowski and Mauss identified the importance of ritual exchange in social inclusion.[38] This offered a powerful analogy with other forms of exchange in Western societies. In some circumstances, we engage in formal and indirect exchange (such as the exchange of presents). In others, we participate in far-reaching patterns of reciprocity, in which the circle of exchange remains incomplete. For example, many employers give privileges to people according to their length of service. Those who have the privileges can justify them, because they were formerly disadvantaged; those who do not have them will benefit in their turn. In the research for *The gift relationship*, Titmuss found that people gave blood not just because they had received blood, but because someone else had received blood, because they might receive blood, or because they might receive some other benefit from the health service. The principle was sufficiently compelling for Titmuss to make it the core of his analysis of social welfare.[39]

I.1.c.ii *Each person must have regard to others.*

Because people do not live in isolation (▶ I.1.a), because their relationships are governed by social norms (▶ I.1.c), and because they are

---

38 M. Mauss (1925) *The gift: forms and functions of exchange in archaic societies*, London: Cohen and West, 1966.

39 R. Titmuss (1970) *The gift relationship*, Harmondsworth: Penguin.

interdependent (▶ I.1.a.i), they must have regard to others. Inevitably, this raises questions about the nature of the obligations each person has to society. The questions which follow were put, long ago, by Hillel, and they are set out in 'The Ethics of the Fathers', part of the Talmud.

I.1.c.ii(1) If I am not for myself, who will be for me?

In some political discourses, people are regarded as fundamentally selfish. 'Self interest, not altruism', we read, 'is mankind's main driving force'.[40] As an explanation of the way in which each person acts, this is profoundly and obviously wrong. The assumption that human behaviour is wholly, or even largely, self-motivated is untenable; family life is the simplest way to refute it.

Hillel's question seems, rhetorically, to invite a sceptical answer. It is tempting to reply 'no one', that the only person you can be sure of is yourself. But that is not the only answer that can be given. My family will be for me, as I will be for them. My community, which is more distant, may be for me, but I am not sure of it; and I may be for them, but I am not very sure of that either. We do not come into the world without social ties. We are born into families and communities. As the distance becomes greater, the sense of responsibility which one feels diminishes – but that is almost a definition of what social 'distance' means. We may expect self-interest, and we may take it for granted, but it is not only through self-interest that people act. Responsibilities extend to family, friends, colleagues, and in some cases even strangers. People in society exhibit both altruism and kinship relations – a rare combination in the animal world, which apparently we share with vampire bats.

I.1.c.ii(2) If I am only for myself, what am I?

Hillel's second question calls attention to the obligations we all have. There is something wrong with people who are only for themselves, and there is a name for them. A person who lacks all sense of obligation to others is a 'psychopath' (or in America, a 'sociopath').[41] As a psychiatric condition, its use is mainly limited to people whose behaviour is sufficiently disturbed to make them dangerous to others. The phenomenon is more common than this suggests, however: the psychopath's lack of emotional engagement and moral insensibility infect some other arenas of real life, including politics and business.

---

40 F. Field (1996) *Stakeholder welfare*, London: IEA Health and Welfare Unit, p. 19.

41 M. Gelder, D. Gath and R. Mayou (1989) *Oxford textbook of psychiatry*, 2nd edition, Oxford: Oxford University Press, ch. 5.

The question refers back to the one before it. If we are not 'only for ourselves', we are also for someone else. If we are for someone else, then for some people the answer to the first question has to include those people who do not accept that being only for themselves is enough.

I.1.c.ii(3)   If not now, when?

Hillel's third question is abrupt and surprising, but the others might be meaningless without it. Obligations to other people are all very well, but we have to do something about them. 'When' matters.

The question seems to call for the answer, 'now'; but now is not the only answer. Many of the obligations we have cut across generations. People support their parents because their parents supported them, and after they have supported their children they may feel that their children have an obligation to support them. (Reciprocity continues to play a role: even when capacities fail, there is a continuing interchange between the generations.)[42] This is not, however, the only source of the obligation, and in the second case especially the position is not strong. Changes in family structures have weakened these obligations – divorce, in particular, raises questions about the definition of the family and the limits of obligation – but they have not obliterated them. There are two other principles at work. People support their parents, not just because their parents supported them, but because their parents supported their grandparents. They support their children, not just because their children will support them, but because their own parents supported them when they were children. The double-headed nature of the obligation – that there is both balanced and generalized exchange – is important, because it means that even where one factor does not apply, the other may still do so. The pattern of obligations is illustrated in Figure 2. Each circle represents a generation; the direction of obligations moves to generations above, to generations below, and reciprocally between successive generations. The figure only shows four generations, but that is arbitrary: the line of obligations can be extended forward or backward indefinitely. The answer to Hillel's question, then, is not just 'now'; it is for the past, the present and the future.

I.1.c.iii   *Obligations have to be counterbalanced with rights.*

The picture which emerges of social obligation is, in many respects, intimidating. If there were only social obligations, there would be little scope for autonomous action. This was the dominant view of feudal society, and it is still central to the Confucian welfare states of South East

---

42 H. Qureshi and A. Walker (1989) *The caring relationship: elderly people and their families*, Basingstoke: Macmillan.

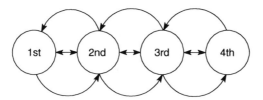

Figure 2   *Obligations between generations*

Asia.[43] The Enlightenment, and the individualist critique it generated, was an attempt to break away from the conservative, confining, suffocating view of society which this view sustained.

The challenge to the established order was framed in terms of rights. Obligations related mainly to the things people had to do, and to the things they could not do; rights were concerned with what they could do, and what others could not do to them. Rights were seen as inherent in an individual, so that each person had something about them which changed the way that others would act towards them. Each person was valuable, and each person was protected. Some rights could be construed from the duties that other people had towards a person, but many could not. Rights included liberties – things which people could do without the interference of others. The US Declaration of Independence proclaimed the right to 'life, liberty and the pursuit of happiness'.

There are conflicts between these principles. Marriage is seen, in Western culture, as a matter of individual choice, and arranged marriages are not generally accepted. I suspect that few parents or children would feel, however, that their child's or parent's choice of partner had nothing to do with them (though they might not make any comment if they thought it would be ineffective or counterproductive). The acceptance of individualism has not led to the removal of obligations, but rather to a softening of them, qualified by other principles.

It is striking how little conventional rights – like freedom of assembly, freedom of worship or freedom of speech – have to do with the obligations that bind us. Although there is a strand in individualism which asserts total independence, not many people would hold that the principle of individual freedom absolves a person of obligations to families, to past or future generations, or to other people.

---

43 Lin Ka (1999) *Confucian welfare cluster*, Tampere, Finland: University of Tampere.

I.2

SOCIETY

I.2 Social relationships are patterned and structured.

Collective action
> I.2.a   *People form groups.*
> I.2.a.i   Social groups are defined by a pattern of relationships within the group.
>> I.2.a.i(1) Social groups are not defined by relationships beyond the group.
> I.2.a.ii People have relationships with groups.
> I.2.a.iii Groups may have relationships with other groups.
> I.2.a.iv Group action is collective action.

Society and social relationships
> I.2.b   *A society is made up of social networks.*
> I.2.b.i   Social cohesion is a function of the strength of social relationships.
> I.2.b.ii Society is constantly changing.
> I.2.b.iii Social relationships are patterned, rather than fixed.
> I.2.b.iv Societies reproduce themselves.

Social structure
> I.2.c   *Societies have a structure.*
> I.2.c.i   The social structure is unequal.
>> I.2.c.i(1) Social relationships are gendered.
>> I.2.c.i(2) Class shapes social relationships, and is shaped by them.
> I.2.c.ii Social structures convey a sense of social division.
>> I.2.c.ii(1) The main divisions in modern societies relate to 'race', ethnicity and nationality.
> I.2.c.iii Where societies are divided, ties of obligation still remain.

Collective action

I.2.a People form groups.

People have relationships with specific combinations of other people. At the risk of some confusion, I am going to use the simplest and most obvious words to describe this process: people form groups. The confusion comes about because we use the word 'group' for lots of different purposes – a pop group, a group of air passengers, an industrial group and so on – and the uses are not always consistent. The groups I am concerned with here are people linked by social relationships. Probably the simplest and clearest example is a family. Other groups acquire such an identity in several ways – through formal structures, like the workplace or school, or through common patterns of behaviour, like the congregation of a church or football fans. Social groups have three core elements: identity, which is based on social recognition of the group; membership, which is the identification of people with the group; and relationships between the group's members.

The issues of identity, membership and relationships are interrelated, and difficult to separate in practice, but relationships are the key. People do not form social groups only because they have something in common. People who have university degrees, play the accordion, or have been admitted to mental institutions are not defined as members of social groups on that account. It is debatable whether communication and interaction are enough in themselves. For example, the Internet is not yet identifiable as a base for social groups, though it is easy to imagine circumstances in which it could be. People form social groups if these issues become a focus for their social relationships, and any of them could be.

I.2.a.i Social groups are defined by a pattern of relationships within the group.

Social groups are defined by a pattern of social relationships – including patterns of communication, interaction, exchange and obligation. This does not mean that every member of the group must have a relationship with every other member. The relationships which exist within a group are complex; there are often many relationships, and networks overlap. A member of the Jewish community will commonly be linked to other members of the community by family relationships, social contact, formal social groupings, voluntary and benevolent activity, and perhaps, occasionally, religious practice.

The relationships within groups are sometimes referred to as a 'network'. The term is expressive: like a net, the lines of communication run both outwards and across each other. Although social networks are complex, they are not random, and there are recognizable patterns of social relationships formed in any society. In Western society, the most obvious of these are the relationships of family, neighbourhood and employment; others include contact through formal education, social groups, ethnic and religious communities. The term 'network' has, perhaps, the unfortunate connotation that there is some pattern or order in the whole structure. There is no reason why there should be, though there are certainly patterns within the whole: relationships formed through family, work, education and community form identifiable systems of communication and interaction.

I.2.a.i(1)   Social groups are not defined by relationships beyond the group.

A common experience is not enough to define a group. Social groups are identified not just by identity and membership, but by relationships between the group's members (▸ I.2.a). Dog owners or the fans of a particular rock band do not constitute a social group. Nor do the victims of rape, for the same reason – though there may be situations in which some victims of rape might declare a common cause. By the same argument, people who have experienced racism are not necessarily linked by that experience. The point is important politically, because there has been a determined attempt by some political groups to identify all victims of racism as 'black', a position which does not relate to the experience or perception of many of those whom it is intended to include.[44]

The relationships which groups have beyond the group can be important for the establishment of a group identity. Identity is part of what defines a social group, and in practice it has often been a starting point for group formation, but it is not sufficient. Children, shopkeepers, people with learning disabilities or women have significant common aspects in their social relationships, but they are not 'social groups' in the sense which is being used here; there can be no expectation of mutual relationships or common action.

I.2.a.ii   People have relationships with groups.

People who participate in a group have a relationship, not just with other members of the group, but with the groups themselves. Where groups are constituted formally, like a mutual aid society or a religious organization, this is easy to see; where they are loosely defined, the relationship is vaguer. People do not usually say they 'have a relationship' with a group, because real people do not talk like that; they are more likely to

---

44 T. Modood (1997) 'Culture and identity', ch. 9 of T. Modood and R. Berthoud (eds) *Ethnic minorities in Britain: diversity and disadvantage*, London: Policy Studies Institute.

say things like, 'I belong here', 'I want to give something to my community', or 'We ought to do something'.

Groups are formed by patterns of relationships within the group. Some of those relationships are held by people, not with other people in the group, but with the group itself. Any obligation which is held generally is held to the group, because the group is identified as the general unit. Conversely, any obligation to a person which is not held specifically by others, but is held in general, is held by the group. The obligation to help others in a community is held generally; it can be expressed, for example, as a desire to help one's home town. Similarly, a general obligation towards people within that community, like old people, will be expressed as the obligation of the community towards its elderly.

I.2.a.iii Groups may have relationships with other groups.

Groups, like people, may have relationships. This can be difficult to picture, because social groups have no actual existence, and having contact with a group member is not the same as having contact with the group. It is not possible to talk to a social group, or to exchange something with them, and talking about groups having relationships sounds like 'reification' – investing an artificial social construct with the status of something real.

There are some exceptions. Some groups are also persons: we can communicate with a business or an institution, and it makes perfectly good sense to say that a business is responsible for the consequences of its actions, even though the business has no mind. Some groups have a strong enough identity to be treated as if they were persons: we can visit a family, share a meal with it, or have obligations to it. (The view of the individual as the natural focus of rights and obligations is, in historical terms, relatively recent; in Roman law it was the family which held property, and both legally and morally there are still many survivals of this principle.)

Can this be extended to other groups? There are many cases in which this is done, though they are controversial. An example is the argument that the United States has special obligations to its indigenous peoples. This would be nonsensical if obligations are held only by individuals to individuals, and yet Robert Nozick – one of the main apostles of individualized rights and obligation – is prepared to accept it.[45] The root of the argument is that groups are connected to people, and to other groups, through the same networks which bind people to each other. The test of whether a group is bound is the same as the test of whether a group exists – the issue of common identification. There is no real distinction to make between the statements that 57,000 businesses from one country trade

---

45 R. Nozick (1974) *Anarchy, state and utopia*, Oxford: Blackwell, p. ix.

with 43,000 in the other, or that two countries are said to be engaged in trade with each other. In both cases the trade takes place, not as the action of isolated individuals, or even of individuals in concert, but in the context of a complex, interlocking system of interdependency; it is not possible to distinguish the roots of obligation solely in relationships between individuals. On that argument, one community can be obliged to another, and nations can have obligations to other nations.

I.2.a.iv Group action is collective action.

Collective action is the action of a social group. It takes three main forms. First, there are actions taken to form groups. Actions which are taken to cement social relationships, including social gatherings and ceremonies like weddings and funerals, are part of what helps to define a group or community. These are collective actions, both in the sense that they are done by a group and because they generate a collective identity.

Second, there is mutualistic action – action which members of the group take for each other. When a group of friends pass gossip to each other, or a group of carers of people with disabilities offer each other aid and support, these are forms of collective action. The action may not be done by everyone in the group. There may be recipients and donors with distinct roles, and there may be many in the group who are not directly affected at a particular time – people who could contribute or benefit, rather than those who do. The action is collective because of its relationship to the identity or nature of the group.

Third, there is concerted action, when people do the same things as others in the group. When a church group meets for worship, or a political group stages a demonstration, these are collective actions. There are many common actions taken by people which are not collective. For example, millions of pensioners watch certain television programmes at regular times, and a very substantial proportion of the world's population can be relied on to tune in to World Cup soccer or the Eurovision Song Contest, but that does not mean they are doing so collectively. Similarly, there are identifiable categories of people who are recognizably following common codes of action, like motorists or shoppers, but their actions are not collective either. There is no necessary relationship between the members of the category, and their actions are not concerted. There has to be a direct link between the nature of the action and the social group.

Society and social relationships

I.2.b   A society is made up of social networks.

It is difficult to define a 'society' precisely. It is not a simple association, and people are not part of it just because they share characteristics with other people. Equally, physical closeness is not enough. People in society are bound in a complex, interlocking web of social relationships (▸ I.2.a.i). Social groups are an important part of these relationships, but they are not the whole story: the networks which make up a society go beyond the relationships of the groups contained within it – they include, for example, personal obligations and obligations to strangers. The French refer to these relationships as relationships of 'solidarity'; Durkheim's famous distinction between 'mechanical' and 'organic' solidarity distinguishes two different kinds of social organization which follow from the development of the division of labour.[46]

Solidarity implies relationships between the members of a society. A society has all the characteristics of a social group: membership, relationships, and identity (▸ I.2.a). In that sense, a society can be represented as a meta-group – a group of groups.

This tends to suggest an overall coherence in the relationships which may not be apparent when the relationships are looked at in any detail. It would be false to suppose that everyone is a part of a social network. People are integrated into society to greater or lesser degrees. Some people have relatively few points of contact – often only with their family, or perhaps with formal social services. These people are referred to as 'marginal', though in French that term also has the unfortunate connotation of deviance or immorality. Others have almost no contact at all, and they are seen as 'excluded'. The issue of social exclusion has become a major concern of the European Union, which has taken powers to respond to exclusion across a wide range of activities.[47]

I.2.b.i   Social cohesion is a function of the strength of social relationships.

The strength of social relationships can be identified with social proximity – not physical nearness, but nearness in the sense of obligations. In close-knit groups there are strongly held expectations, patterns of generalized exchange and powerful social sanctions for a breach of expectations (▸ I.1.c.i). The effect is to hold society together – to tie the parts together. This is 'social cohesion'.

---

46 E. Durkheim (1915) *The division of labor in society*, trans. G. Simpson, New York: Free Press, 1964.

47 E.g. Commission of the European Communities (1993) *Medium term action programme to control exclusion and promote solidarity*, COM(93) 435; Commission of the European Communities (1994) *European social policy – a way forward for the Union* (White Paper), COM(94) 333 final; Commission of the European Communities (1995) *Final report on the implementation of the Community programme concerning the economic and social integration of the economically and socially less privileged groups in society*, COM (95)94 final.

One of the most extreme forms of sanction is ostracism, or deliberate exclusion from the group. Parents who disinherit children, associations which expel members and nationalities which stigmatize foreigners are engaging in a similar kind of activity: the establishment of social borders. There are, however, societies in which there are strong borders with only a limited degree of social cohesion – the United States is the most obvious example – and it is difficult to avoid the conclusion that strong boundaries are not sufficient to promote cohesion. Are they necessary? The example of the family suggests that they are not; strong families are well able to accept new members and changing boundaries, while the effect of expulsion from the family may be to fracture rather than reinforce the unit. Cohesion is, then, a function of the strength of relationships, not of the strength of borders. (This is consonant with the criteria used to define the nature of social groups: groups are defined by the relationships within them, not beyond them: ▶ I.2.a.i).

I.2.b.ii Society is constantly changing.

Society can be understood as an association, but its nature is not fixed. A society consists of a complex series of interlocking relationships. These relationships form social networks, which overlap and intertwine. Some relationships are fairly constant – though even the family, once the stable core of social relationships, has been the subject of extensive change in recent years. Others change relatively rapidly: friendships, neighbourhoods, the workplace are all likely to change several times during a person's lifetime.

I.2.b.iii Social relationships are patterned, rather than fixed.

The very terms in which this has been expressed point to the existence of consistent patterns in social interaction. The core elements of social contact remain, for most people, family, the neighbourhood and the workplace. This is not necessarily true, because other patterns of life are possible. Everyday living can be built about a household, rather than a family; communities can be built about common links, like those of race or religion, rather than geographical location; social interaction and involvement might be based on a different type of common experience, like education or military service. (Political discourse in East Asia is often based on a conception of the country, and the political community, analogous to a family, or at least to a family group.)[48] But there should be some kind of pattern, because otherwise it can be very difficult to maintain the contact and relationships we need in order to manage in

---

48 Lin Ka (1999).

society. My research has included work with psychiatric patients, whose patterns of relationships have been disrupted.[49] Psychiatric patients who were being treated in hospital or community settings tended to have few major interactions, but in general they did retain contact at least with their families. The psychiatric patients in the research who were homeless, by contrast, had often lost contact with everyone, including their families; without support, they were plunged into a limbo where it was difficult to get the necessities of everyday life – including food, warmth and shelter. Patterned relationships, like those of family, community and religion, offer a degree of stability and security in a shifting environment. Social order means, not that things cease to change, but that patterns are maintained despite changes.

I.2.b.iv   Societies reproduce themselves.

A striking feature in these patterns is the apparent ability of societies to reproduce themselves, leading to similar patterns in subsequent generations. 'Reproduction' is not like the reproduction of a picture, faithful in every detail. It is more like the reproduction of a family. New generations are born and grow; they are socialized into the norms and culture prevalent in society. Reproduction is essential to the continuation of any society; it produces the next generation, the next workforce, the next parents, the next set of taxpayers.

The apparent stability of the process of reproduction is partly illusory, both because reproduction is taking place in a changing environment, and because societies are not really the same from one generation to the next; but part of the process is stable, because children move into social circumstances which are often closely related to those of their parents. In some societies (particularly traditional caste societies) the opportunities and life chances of children are fixed, or 'ascribed', at birth, but this is not really the case in developed contemporary societies. The study of social mobility focuses on the changing economic and social position of children relative to their parents, but the very existence of such an area of study presumes that something about this change is worthy of note: there is an implicit assumption that what is true for one generation will, other things being equal, be true for the next. This is not necessarily what happens: although parental status is a powerful determinant of life chances, several other factors are also influential – gender, education and marriage being prominent amongst them. Poor children are more likely than others to become poor adults, but they are not destined to be poor;

---

49 N. Crockett and P. Spicker (1994) *Discharged: homelessness among psychiatric patients in Scotland*, Edinburgh: Shelter (Scotland); P. Spicker, I. Anderson, R. Freeman and R. McGilp (1995) 'Discharged into the community: the experience of psychiatric patients', *Social Services Research*, 1: 27–35.

research on intergenerational continuity has shown that most poor children do not continue in poverty, and the effect of employment opportunities, and marriage with people who are not poor, means that there is surprisingly little direct continuity across generations.[50]

Much more important is the stability of the framework, or pattern, in which people find themselves. Life chances are not fixed, but the kinds of opportunities which children will have are patterned by the society they grow up in. The social structure affects the housing people live in, the education they undergo, the social contacts they will form, and the kinds of occupation which will be available to them. It has, then, a profound effect on their lives. Reproduction takes place in the context of structured social relationships, and this gives the (potentially misleading) impression of stable, ordered development.

Social structure

I.2.c Societies have a structure.

Generalizations about society are concerned with patterns, rather than direct causal links; few statements about social processes are true for everyone, or even for most people. It may be true, for example, that taller people are often seen in more favourable terms than shorter people,[51] but this does not mean that most tall people are seen more favourably; it is simply a factor, which has to be balanced against other factors. Sociological statements tend to be concerned with trends, probabilities or tendencies rather than fixed relationships. Arguments about family structure, racial discrimination or educational disadvantage are based on the analysis of general patterns of this type.

Describing society as a structure implies that some elements have a definable relationship to others. At first sight this may seem implausible, because in a complex, overlapping system of social networks the relationship of each element to others is liable to constant change. The argument that such patterns form a structure is, necessarily, a question of interpretation, and some sociologists – mainly the 'phenomenologists' – have made a comfortable living by arguing for deconstruction of such concepts. The central argument for a structured analysis is simply that a range of topics – including, amongst others, the distribution of income,

---

50 A.B. Atkinson, A. Maynard and C. Trinder (1983) *Parents and children,* London: Heinemann; I. Kolvin, F.J.W. Miller, D.M. Scott, S.R.M. Gatzanis and M. Fleeting (1990) *Continuities of deprivation? The Newcastle 1000 family study,* Aldershot: Avebury.

51 K. Deaux and L. Wrightsman (1988) *Social psychology,* Pacific Grove, CA: Brookes/Cole, pp. 95–97.

health or education[52] – are more effectively dealt with by structured analysis than by phenomenology.

I.2.c.i The social structure is unequal.

Although social relationships are patterned, they are also complex, and differentiated. People play many roles, including for example roles within a family, occupational roles and roles within a community (▶ I.1.a.ii). These roles carry different expectations, and so different combinations of rights and obligations. Rights and obligations, in turn, are commonly related to differences in social esteem. The mechanisms are not straightforward, because there are cases in which social position is not related to social action. The effect of adopting differentiated roles is, obviously enough, that people's social positions differ. They do not, however, differ randomly; rank has its privileges, and commonly social position, or status, is associated with the structure of opportunities and rewards in a society. The social structure is unequal, not simply because people are in different positions, but because the pattern of relationships places them in positions of relative advantage or disadvantage.

Social status consists of a set of expectations, and so of social obligations (▶ I.1.c). Status is sometimes identified with roles, which are patterned expectations; equally, it can be identified with rights and obligations, which are also forms of patterned expectation. Some sociologists have argued that status is simply a constellation of roles, a collection of rights and duties.[53] This may be true of some statuses, but not of all. Some statuses, including nobility and illegitimacy, are ascribed to people by birth, and no clear role is attached. Some attach to achievements, like professional competence or success in business, and if there are rights and obligations attached they seem to relate to the activity rather than to the status attached to it.

It is true, though, that status is linked to roles and obligations. The status of the aristocrat derived initially from the role of warrior, then from that of landowner; the status of the doctor relates to professional competence and obligations. (Many minor professions, including teachers, social workers and nurses, have tried to emulate the position of doctors by imitating their professional structure and norms.)[54] The mechanism by which the link is established is disputed. Weber described

---

52 D. Champerknowne and F. Cowell (1998) *Economic inequality and income distribution*, Cambridge: Cambridge University Press; P. Townsend, N. Davidson and M. Whitehead (1988) *Inequalities in health*, Harmondsworth: Penguin; A. Furlong (1997) 'Education and the reproduction of class-based inequalities', in H. Jones (ed.) *Towards a classless society?* London: Routledge.

53 R. Linton (1936) *The study of man*, New York: Appleton-Century.

54 P. Wilding (1982) *Professional power and social welfare*, London: Routledge and Kegan Paul.

status as a form of social honour.[55] Some theorists have seen this as esteem given in return for services rendered,[56] others as a cruder reflection of economic position.[57]

It is possible to link this analysis to a concept of social power.[58] Whether power means the ability to produce intended effects,[59] or even the potential that someone has to affect the behaviour of others,[60] the nature of obligation means that many people have it. Power is a relational concept: that is, it has to be understood in terms of the behaviour of people in relation to each other. Wherever there are differential obligations, people have power over others. These relationships have to be understood in the context of a social framework in which people are unequal. Power, like status, can be structured; some people are able to direct the conduct of others who accept that direction.

I.2.c.i(1) Social relationships are gendered.

Another form of structural inequality differentiates the sexes. The statement that social relationships are 'gendered' is intended to convey the idea that gender differentials are a basic element in the pattern of social networks. Gender determines many of the roles which men and women play, their opportunities and life chances. Gender is written all the way through social networks, like 'Blackpool' in a stick of rock, and any analysis which is based on those networks, particularly at the interpersonal level, is likely to reflect issues related to gender structures. Gøsta Esping-Andersen has argued that gender relationships and changes in family structures are the key to understanding recent changes in economic and social structures in developed countries.[61]

The root of gender inequality rests, like inequalities of status, in differentiation between roles, and in the relative esteem which is attached to

---

55 M. Weber (1967) 'The development of caste', in R. Bendix and S.M. Lipset (eds) *Class, status and power*, 2nd edition, London: Routledge and Kegan Paul, pp. 31–32.

56 G. Homans (1961) *Social behaviour: its elementary forms*, London: Routledge and Kegan Paul; P. Blau (1964) *Exchange and power in social life*, New York: John Wiley and Sons.

57 W.G. Runciman (1963) *Social science and political theory*, Cambridge: Cambridge University Press.

58 G. Homans (1961) *Social behaviour: its elementary forms*, London: Routledge and Kegan Paul; P. Blau (1964) *Exchange and power in social life*, New York: John Wiley.

59 B. Russell (1960) *Power*, London: Unwin.

60 S. Lukes (1978) 'Power and authority', in T. Bottomore and R. Nisbet (eds) *A history of sociological analysis*, London: Heinemann.

61 G. Esping-Andersen (1999) 'Micro-sociological determinants of economic change'. Address to European Sociological Association, Amsterdam.

those roles. The inequality of male and female puts women at a disadvantage in several important dimensions of social life – notably education,[62] work opportunities[63] and income.[64] Beyond this, though, the obligations which apply to people differ according to their gender: mothers have stronger obligations to care for children than fathers, and in Western countries daughters (and even daughters-in-law) may have stronger obligations to care for elderly people than sons do.[65]

I.2.c.i(2)   Class shapes social relationships, and is shaped by them.

A third form of inequality is inequality of resources, usually expressed in terms of income and wealth. People who are in a poorer economic position are disadvantaged relative to those in superior economic positions; a person with more money is able to exercise more choice on that account, and in conditions of scarcity a person with more money can purchase items before someone with less money. This is different from the inequalities of status or gender, because unlike them it is not directly attributable to the structure of social relationships. People may be rich because of high status, but they can also have high status because they are rich. Income and wealth reflect the structure of relationships, but they also help to shape them; the factors interact.

Classes, according to Weber, 'are groups of people who, from the standpoint of specific interests, have the same economic position'.[66] Class has a range of other meanings in sociology,[67] but for the purposes of this argument this is a convenient shorthand. People with different commands of resources live differently: they are able to buy different things, to live in different places, to pursue different activities. The common patterns which this describes are the patterns of social class.

---

62 P. Mayes (1989) *Gender*, London: Longman, ch. 3; G. Pascall (1997) *Social policy: a new feminist analysis*, London: Routledge, ch. 4.

63 C. Callender (1996) 'Women and employment', in C. Hallett (ed.) *Women and social policy*, Hemel Hempstead: Prentice-Hall; S. Lonsdale (1992) 'Patterns of paid work', in C. Glendinning and J. Millar (eds) *Women and poverty in Britain – the 1990s*, Hemel Hempstead: Harvester Wheatsheaf.

64 Glendinning and Millar (1992); J. Millar (1996) 'Women, poverty and social security', in Hallett (1996).

65 G. Dalley (1988) *Ideologies of caring*, Basingstoke: Macmillan; S. Baldwin and J. Twigg (1990) 'Women and community care', in M. McLean and D. Groves, *Women's issues in social policy*, London: Routledge. Contrast S. Chen (1996) *Social policy of the economic state and community care in Chinese culture*, Aldershot: Ashgate.

66 M. Weber (1967) 'The development of caste', in R. Bendix and S.M. Lipset, *Class, status and power*, London: Routledge and Kegan Paul, pp. 31–32.

67 S. Edgell (1993) *Class*, London: Routledge.

Classes are not 'groups' in the sense in which that term was used earlier (▶ I.2.a). Home owners[68] or people with disabilities[69] might be identified as classes in terms of their economic position, but identity is not enough to make a group: it does not imply mutual relationships or common action. The significance of class as a concept rests in what it conveys about people's relative social position: the patterns of behaviour associated with class shape life chances, opportunities, occupational roles and status. Class and status are interrelated.

Class does not mean the same thing in every society. Like the myth of the individual (▶ I.1.b.ii), the myth of class consciousness has mattered in different times and places; it is important when people believe in it, and act as if it is true, and relatively unimportant when they do not. Understood as differences in economic position, classes are a major element of social relationships, whatever the society; but relationships within classes, and between them, depend on a range of social factors, and their importance varies.

I.2.c.ii   Social structures convey a sense of social division.

Reference to a society as 'divided' runs the risk of internal contradiction. If a society was truly divided, with clear borders running between different groups, it would not be one society, but several. Some societies have come to be divided literally, but more typically the division is imagined; cultural, linguistic and racial differences are taken to determine patterns of social contact and interaction, with the effect that the divisions become self-perpetuating.

Although social divisions might be generated by inequality, social division is not the same as inequality. Men and women are unequal, in the sense that women are disadvantaged socially relative to men; but, whatever the differences between the sexes, there is too much interaction for it to be possible to talk meaningfully about a 'division'. Inequalities in income and wealth do not lead directly to social divisions, because the inequality coexists with a system of interwoven obligations – though it has been argued that, at the extremes, 'economic distance' leads to effective exclusion from social networks.[70] Similarly, there is no true division between social classes – though caste societies have something like a division in their reaction to pariah castes, who are not allowed to

---

68 E.g. J. Rex and R. Moore (1967) *Race, community and conflict*, Oxford: Oxford University Press.

69 P. Townsend (1979) *Poverty in the United Kingdom*, Harmondsworth: Penguin.

70 M. O'Higgins and S. Jenkins (1990) 'Poverty in the EC: 1975, 1980, 1985', in R. Teekens and B. van Praag (eds) *Analysing poverty in the European Community* (*Eurostat News* special edition 1–1990), Luxembourg: European Communities.

marry, work with or even stand next to people from other castes.[71] This is a case in which distance is compounded by the distinct identification of a social group, and it can be argued that identification is crucial to the nature of social divisions.

A sense of social division seems to come about when some groups have such a strong sense of identity, and such strong borders, that they exclude contact and interaction with other groups; the breakup of the former Yugoslavia is a chilling example. Divisions of this kind – based on race, language or culture – commonly reflect a historical inheritance. (This is not enough to explain the resurgence of national or cultural affiliations which had long been dormant. Scottish nationalism or the revival of the Catalan language, for example, have built on historical identity as the basis for a political movement.)

I.2.c.ii(1)   The main divisions in modern societies relate to 'race', ethnicity and nationality.

Social division is intimately bound up with the question of identity, and contemporary identity is primarily expressed in terms of 'race', ethnicity and nationality.

'Race' is frequently referred to in this context, though it is a much vaguer concept than it at first appears; it conflates aspects of biology, ethnicity, skin colour, culture, religion and nationality, none of which is firmly or clearly defined. People of different 'races' are often socially rejected and stigmatized; in the UK and US this is principally defined in terms of colour,[72] in France it relates to Arabs,[73] and in much of central Europe the strongest rejection is of 'gypsies' or travellers.[74]

The concept of ethnicity is closely related to this. Ethnicity refers to cultural differences which distinguish one community from another; gypsies are a prime example.[75] Linguistic differences and tribal affiliations may be significant. Religion is another principal distinguishing factor, and it plays a role similar to race. The division of Protestant and

---

71 E. Leach (ed.) (1960) *Aspects of caste in South India, Ceylon and North-west Pakistan*, Cambridge: Cambridge University Press.

72 P. Baker, L. Anderson and D. Dorn (eds) (1993) *Social problems*, New York: Wadsworth, ch. 8; I. Law (1996) *Racism, ethnicity and social policy*, Hemel Hempstead: Prentice-Hall.

73 A. Policar (1992) 'Racisme et antiracisme: un réexamen, in G. Ferréol (ed.) *Intégration et exclusion dans la société française contemporaine*, Lille: Presses Universitaires de Lille.

74 A. Meszaros and J. David (1990) 'Gipsy disadvantage and social policy in Hungary', in S. Mitra (ed.) *Politics of positive discrimination*, Bombay: Sangam Books.

75 Meszaros and David (1990); D. Hawes and B. Perez (1995) *The gypsy and the state*, Bristol: SAUS.

Catholic in Northern Ireland is analogous; and in certain countries prejudice against Muslims or Jews has been the dominant expression of racism. (In Britain and France the distinction between Muslims and others is a major source of disadvantage, arguably rather more important than any racial difference.)[76]

Nationality is a different source of division, because although it is overlaid with the same kind of stigma as 'race' it also has a legal foundation. Foreign nationals tend to be treated differently from people who have full rights of residence; their rates of pay, tenure of employment, and rights to ownership of property can legitimately be different from that of citizens of the country. The position of guest workers in Germany is illustrative.

The effect of these distinctions is not just to identify groups, but to mark out the borders between them. 'Race' often defines an out-group – a set of people who form social groups and networks, distinct from the in-group. Usually (but not always) the out-group is in a minority. Often, too, the out-group can be directly identified – by skin colour, appearance, clothing or the distinct location of accommodation.

I.2.c.iii   *Where societies are divided, ties of obligation still remain.*

Obligations continue to exist across social divisions. This is virtually a tautology; if there were no relationships running across social boundaries, and no ties of obligation, there would be two societies, not one. Even where there are strong social borders, like the divisions of a caste society, there are generally principles which govern relationships across the boundaries. At the same time, the obligations which extend across social divides are often tenuous. It is in the nature of a social divide that it reduces contact and makes casual interaction less frequent. I argued before that the effect of contact and interaction was to generate relationships, from which obligations flowed (► I.1.c). By the same argument, the effect of reducing contact and insulating some people from an in-group is to diminish the strength of such obligations, and sometimes the obligations which are recognized beyond the group are tenuous. Responsibilities to foreign nationals, for example, tend to be limited.

---

76 Modood (1997); Policar (1992).

SOLIDARITY

I.3 Solidarity is intrinsic to society.

Solidarity: altruism and responsibility
I.3.a	*Altruism is founded in solidarity.*
I.3.a.i	Responsibility diminishes with social distance.
I.3.a.ii	Social obligations extend to strangers.
I.3.a.iii	Helping others is basic social conduct.

Mutual aid
I.3.b	*People who act rationally act collectively.*
I.3.b.i	Mutual aid benefits the participants.
I.3.b.ii	Collective action increases the potential of each person.
I.3.b.iii	Individual interests can conflict with collective action.
	I.3.b.iii(1) Free riders may be compelled to participate in collective action.
	I.3.b.iii(2) Collective action does not have to be compulsory.
I.3.b.iv	Collective action and mutual aid develop spontaneously in society.

Cohesion and exclusion
I.3.c	*Solidarity is an integral aspect of social cohesion.*
I.3.c.i	Collective action defines a community.
I.3.c.ii	Collective action is exclusive as well as inclusive.
I.3.c.iii	Exclusion prevents social integration.
I.3.c.iv	Exclusion limits social cohesion.

Social responsibility and social borders
I.3.d	*Obligations may extend beyond borders.*
I.3.d.i	Solidarity is local and national.
I.3.d.ii	Social responsibility is not confined to national boundaries.

Solidarity: altruism and responsibility

I.3.a Altruism is founded in solidarity.

Altruism is behaviour for the benefit of other people, and it is usually assumed to be motivated by a selfless concern for other people. Richard Titmuss sought to locate social welfare provision in 'ultra obligations', obligations we may feel to others on the basis of generalized principles, even though there was no contact, and no specific duty.[77] This argument has generally been criticized, because it is difficult to identify any altruistic action from which the giver does not, in some sense, benefit – even if it is only through a sense of self-satisfaction – and so which cannot be said in some way to be self-motivated. Relatively few discussions in the academic literature now consider 'altruism' in this sense; it has become more common to see references to 'solidarity'. Solidarity, in the teaching of the Catholic Church, is understood as

> a firm and persevering determination to commit oneself to the common good, that is . . . the good of all and of each individual, because we are all really responsible for each other.[78]

The idea refers to the sense of obligation and responsibility which people feel towards each other. In the last century, solidarity was mainly used to justify collaborative mutual aid, in the form of social insurance. In recent times it has increasingly come to refer to obligations which extend to other people in society, whether or not those other people have made any contribution in their turn.

Solidaristic actions are not straightforwardly altruistic. They can be motivated by reciprocity and social obligation; they may reflect the simple fact of social interdependence; they may reflect religious principle, which is primarily a duty to God rather than to other people. Altruistic actions are an aspect of social solidarity, and they are generated by and through the same principles – social expectations, norms and obligations.

I.3.a.i *Responsibility diminishes with social distance.*

Solidaristic obligations are not held equally by everyone. Within families, Sahlins argues that relationships are characterized by generalized exchange (► I.1.c.i); the support which family members give each other

---

77 R.M. Titmuss (1970) *The gift relationship*, Harmondsworth: Penguin.
78 Cited in N. Coote (1989) 'Catholic social teaching', *Social Policy and Administration*, 23 (2): 157.

cannot be based on a calculation of costs and benefits.[79] At the same time, obligations towards others are often specific to certain classes of relationship – most notably, the obligations of spouses and of women in the family. There is an element of reciprocity in such relationships, but that would not of itself explain why men should be obliged less than women, or why daughters-in-law should have responsibility for parents-in-law; clearly, what is happening is that a range of social norms, rather than one dominant norm, govern family conduct.

The principle of generalized reciprocity extends to the relationship between generations beyond the family (► I.1.c.i; I.1.c.ii(3)). Elderly people and children have acquired a special status which legitimizes the receipt of social welfare services. One basis for supporting educational provision is that people have received education and now have an obligation to help others receive it. The basis for most pension schemes is that people contribute for the benefit of pensioners now, in the expectation that the succeeding generation will help them in their turn. Clearly, the relationship is more remote than it would be within the family; Sahlins suggests that the relationship with more remote social contacts is more likely to be characterized by balanced exchange. People who give to friends and acquaintances are likely to expect something in return. Where social contacts are more distant, exchange becomes 'negative'; the character of generalized and balanced exchange begins more directly to reflect the concerns of self-interest. We owe a greater duty to those who are most near to us, and the least duty to those who are furthest away; that is part of what 'nearness' means.

I.3.a.ii Social obligations extend to strangers.

Even for strangers, however, social interaction is governed by obligations. Obligations are a form of social norm, and norms consist of expectations about behaviour, coupled with some sanction for non-compliance (► I.1.c). Some obligations are stronger than others. Because close social proximity is associated with higher levels of interaction and obligation, obligations which relate to strangers tend to be weaker; but they are still there. Some obligations are negative, like the demand not to interfere, not to do things which will jeopardize someone's position unnecessarily (like driving a car straight at them), or to respect a person's personal space or possessions. Some, however, are positive. In the United States, 'Good Samaritan laws' have had to be passed to remove the threat of penalties for helping people; in France, by contrast, the law makes it a criminal offence not to assist a person in distress or danger. Irrespective of the legal issues, the French approach seems to me to reflect more accurately the most widely held moral position; most

---

79 M. Sahlins (1974) *Stone age economics*, London: Tavistock.

people would disapprove of someone who failed to help another person, and in many cases there is a positive obligation to do so.

I.3.a.iii   Helping others is basic social conduct.

In the literature of psychology, the term 'altruism' is treated as a sub-category of 'prosocial behaviour', action which is done for the benefit of others.[80] People help other people in a variety of ways; motivations, like altruism, charity and humanitarianism, are difficult to identify, but the process of helping itself is not. Whether the action is minor, like holding a door open for someone else, or significant, including devoting oneself to caring for another person, life is full of examples of people helping others. Interdependence is routine. Some prosocial behaviour is so deeply internalized that we do not even think about it. 'Good manners' sometimes call for simple acts of prosocial behaviour, such as giving a drink to a visitor, or giving way to other road users, or holding a door open for a stranger; the person who fails to do so is not just selfish, but a boor. This means that people can engage in behaviour which appears to be altruistic, without having any consciously altruistic motivation. People give to others, or support others – most obviously, in the relationships between parents and children – without moving to think about the potential benefits.

Where the motivation becomes conscious, a wide range of factors come into play. Part of the process which is thought of as altruism is explained in terms of reciprocity. If people do not look for a direct and immediate return, but only to take part in a general circle of exchange (▶ I.1.c.i), there is no social action which might not in some sense eventually work to the benefit of the donor. There may be examples of purely self-denying altruism, but they are not part of the fabric of everyday life. This is not to deny the possibility of sainthood, but this book is not about sainthood, and those who want to become saints should read something else.

Mutual aid

I.3.b   People who act rationally act collectively.

Much economic theory is built around the analysis of the behaviour of rational, self-interested individuals. In economic theory, the rational person is an artificial construct, designed to show the implications of different patterns of decision-making. Each individual maximizes utility,

---

80 H. Bierhoff (1996) 'Prosocial behaviour', in M. Hewstone, W. Stroebe and G. Stephenson (eds) *Introduction to social psychology*, Oxford: Blackwell.

which means that individuals choose what they most prefer.[81] Utility is not necessarily selfish, but the effect of defining it in individualistic terms has been to identify rational behaviour with self-interest; economists have depended on the association with self-interest to justify the assumption of utility maximization (rather than satisfaction). Adam Smith wrote, famously, that 'It is not from the benevolence of the butcher, the brewer, or the baker that we expect our dinner, but from their regard to their own interest.'[82]

This is sometimes identified, mistakenly, with the fallacy that people's actions are wholly self-interested (▸ I.1.c.ii(1)). Economic analysis is concerned not with the explanation of human behaviour in all its forms, but in the analysis of how that behaviour changes in response to economic stimuli. Economic behaviour takes place in a social context; often there are strong obligations and precepts in place before economic choices are made.

There are important reasons why rational individuals should behave collectively. Collective behaviour is group behaviour (▸ I.2.a.iv), and at first blush group behaviour seems to be the antithesis of the actions of the self-interested, economic individual. The argument that the 'rational individual' acts collectively does not mean that only collective actions are rational, but simply that in some circumstances the rational individual will opt for collective, rather than individual, action. The focus of this argument falls mainly on mutualistic action.

The arguments for mutualistic behaviour have been explored by some writers through a particular form of game theory, depending on the 'prisoner's dilemma'.[83] The basic scenario of the prisoner's dilemma assumes that there are two people under arrest for a crime, and each is asked to inform on the other. If both remain silent, they will get only a light sentence; if both confess, both go to gaol; but if one confesses while the other does not, then the one who remains silent will have a heavier sentence, while the other will go free. The greatest benefits, conse-quently, are gained through co-operation, but this depends on trust. The greatest penalty lies in trusting another person who betrays you. There are lessons to be learned from this kind of analysis – in particular, that where there is a choice, reciprocity is likely to be more productive than treachery.[84] It is difficult, however, to ground the theory – to prove that situations which parallel the 'prisoner's dilemma' happen regularly or

---

81 P. Samuelson and W. Nordhaus (1995) *Economics*, 15th edition, New York: McGraw-Hill, p. 73.

82 A. Smith (1776) *The wealth of nations*, London: Everyman, 1991, p. 13.

83 E.g. G. Axelrod (1990) *The evolution of co-operation*, Harmondsworth: Penguin; R. Frank (1994) *Microeconomics and behavior*, New York: McGraw-Hill, ch. 7; A. de Swaan (1988) *In the care of the state*, Cambridge: Polity.

84 Axelrod (1990).

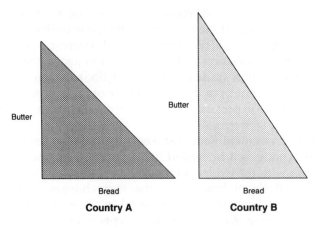

Figure 3   *Comparative advantage*

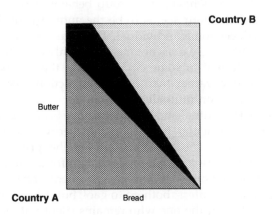

Figure 4   *The benefits of exchange*

frequently in real life. For mutual action to take place, there has to be a real prospect of mutual benefit.

This is the issue addressed by another formal argument, the idea of 'comparative advantage'. It is explained in its simplest form in the field of international economics. If two countries specialize their production and exchange their goods, they can achieve more than either can on its own. Figure 3 shows the potential production of two commodities, bread and butter.

Acting independently, there is a limit to what each country can achieve – a 'production possibility frontier'. Exchange makes it possible for each country to go beyond this frontier. This is shown in Figure 4, by turning the graph for Country B upside down on Country A. There is a new area, marked in black, in the centre of the box. Before specialization and exchange, no part of that area would be accessible; after specialization and exchange, any combination from inside that area is possible. Both parties stand to benefit, because some of the combinations make it possible for both to have more.

Exactly the same principle applies to production and exchange by people within a society. If two rational, utility-maximizing individuals have different productive potentials – for example, in choices between plumbing and bricklaying, or gardening and cooking – they can achieve more through specialization and mutual exchange than they can individually. The proof that this does have an application in society is that there is, in practice, a division of labour: people accept specialized roles within an agreed framework or common objective, and the division of labour is participated in by everyone who has a job.

There are potential problems, and some limitations to the scope of this argument. There is no guarantee of an equitable distribution of gains – one party can be made better off at the expense of another. The production possibility frontier does not have to be straight, and there may be distributions in which both parties would be worse off. The scope for gain may be very limited where there are pronounced inequalities between the parties. Further, the differentiation of status and class implicit in specialization may lead to disadvantage: the clearest example is the division of labour within the home, where the activities undertaken by women have been associated with lower status and power. The central principle, though, is difficult to dispute: that there are potential gains from collaborative action. That is why rational actors will seek to collaborate.

This is the core of the argument for mutualistic action. Mutual aid is essentially a form of collaboration, and the pooling of skills and resources – for example, self-build housing associations, local exchange schemes or babysitting circles – can be expressed in terms of comparative advantage. Pooled resources increase the potential returns to group members – not just because of economies of scale, but because there is an increase in the range of potential outcomes. The same principle extends to many forms of reciprocal action, including reciprocity within families, and to reciprocity over time. The pattern of exchange and interdependency described earlier is social (▶ I.1.c.i), but it can also be justified rationally.

The main limitation of this proof, of course, is that most people are not self-interested utility-maximizers of the kind envisaged in economic theory. They are socialized into the acceptance of social codes, and participation in collective action, which means that they act in a different way, and by different standards.

I.3.b.i *Mutual aid benefits the participants.*

In many cases, mutual aid and solidarity take a specific, specialized form: the pooling of resources for security. The arguments for this kind of action depend on a second set of propositions, which concern the benefits of pooling risks. People's reaction to risks varies, and is difficult to explain in rational terms; many people accept considerable risks to their health or safety (for example, through smoking or riding motor-cycles) while shying away from risks which are extremely remote (like contracting Creutzfeldt-Jakob disease from beef or being subject to terrorist attacks in foreign countries). When individuals make decisions about risks, they take several considerations into account. Part of their decision is based on the perceived level of risk, which is complicated because it is formed of a series of interrelated considerations: the abso-lute level of risk, the level of risk over time, and the marginal level of risk. People know that smoking cigarettes or taking heroin is dangerous, but many think they can get away with it this time, or that they can give it up next month. Part is based on the seriousness of the risk. Small risks with potentially very high costs may be avoided when high risks with lower costs are accepted. Part, too, relates to the perceived alternatives. The risks of motoring are high, but the alternative to using cars in some European societies is not to try to buy food. On the other side of the balance, there is the perceived benefit. The risks of pregnancy, relative to many other conditions, are high, but the benefits of pregnancy are clear and strong. People do not avoid risk; they avoid serious, unnecessary risks if they think the benefits are too small. The central issue is, then, the management of risk, rather than risk avoidance.

Pooling risks, like insurance against theft or ill health, has the main benefit of security; it makes expenses predictable and manageable. The benefit of security is felt, not only by recipients, but by all participants. The calculation of whether this is worthwhile depends on the extent to which people discount risks; the principal evidence that the benefit outweighs the cost is given by the number of people who do it. Volun-tary systems of social insurance have functioned in many countries, often covering most of the population in stable employment: examples are the scheme for unemployment insurance in Denmark,[85] the union-based health service in Israel[86] or the supplementary insurance for sickness offered by mutual societies in France.[87]

---

85 J. Kvist (1997) 'Retrenchment or restructuring? The emergence of a multitiered welfare state in Denmark', in J. Clasen (ed.) *Social insurance in Europe*, Bristol: Policy Press.

86 U. Yanay (1990) 'Service delivery by a trade union – does it pay?', *Journal of Social Policy*, 19 (2): 221–234.

87 H. Bolderson and D. Mabbett (1997) *Delivering social security: a cross-national study*, London: Department of Social Security.

I.3.b.ii Collective action increases the potential of each person.

The theory of comparative advantage shows that productive potential of individuals is increased by specialization and exchange. Mutual aid makes it possible to constrain the impact of risk, and so permit more risky strategies. Collective action permits the pooling of skills, so that each person can draw on the skills of others. Group formation develops possibilities for action, and some things can only be done by many people working in concert. Collective action, consequently, increases potential.

This is all subject to an important reservation. Although it is fairly obvious that some things can only be done through collective action, it is also obvious that some forms of collective action – such as the constraints of authoritarian and theocratic communities – can reduce individual potential. This is because the freedom to act of some people can constrain others, and concern about this potential for constraint is a central argument in the defence of liberty.

I.3.b.iii Individual interests can conflict with collective action.

Mancur Olson argues that everyone is likely to reach a point at which it is in their interest to default from collective action.[88] If people act collectively to provide public facilities like roads or parks, then a rational self-interested individual may consider that it is in his interests to have a 'free ride', taking advantage of the collective action of others. The effect of defaulting may be to increase the costs for those who continue to act collectively, and to increase the incentive for others to default. (This depends, of course, on the view that such an action would not jeopardize the continued existence of coverage, which is uncertain; the judgement is based, again, on an assessment of the situation. There may also be a penalty for defaulting: people who drop out of pension schemes often lose financially, and the first person to show a light in a wartime blackout is also the person who is most likely to be bombed.)[89]

The problem of the 'free rider' is much less acute than Olson's analysis suggests. Sugden argues that his position is manifestly inconsistent with what we know about social behaviour; people do not, for example, stop giving to charity because other people do.[90] Stone points to a series of motivations which encourage people to collective action: the common

88 M. Olson (1971) *The logic of collective action: public goods and the theory of groups*, Cambridge, MA: Harvard University Press.

89 O. Widegren (1997) 'Social solidarity and social exchange', *Sociology*, 31 (4): 755–771.

90 Cited in A. Culyer (1991) 'The normative economics of health care: finance and provision', in A. McGuire, P. Fenn and K. Mayhew (eds) *Providing health care*, Oxford: Oxford University Press.

influences to which people are subject socially, the rewards of co-operation, and, more subtly, the ambiguity of political definitions of problems, which can lead to people understanding their interests in different ways.[91] Many will happily identify the preservation of the collective environment, rather than their individual right to pollute it, as representing the true definition of their interests.

The general point is still valid: individual interests may conflict with collective ones, even if people do sometimes act collectively. A person who is pursuing individual interests may not wish to be tied to collective action. Defaulting from mutual aid seems to be more immediately in the interest of certain individuals, particularly those with high security or low risks. In that light, it is interesting to note that in countries where people have had the choice of whether or not to join social insurance schemes, the vast majority have done so. It is also noteworthy that many of the people who default in practice do so, not because their risks are low, but on the contrary because they are insecure – if they have low income, they cannot afford to participate fully.

I.3.b.iii(1)   Free riders may be compelled to participate in collective action.

Olson sees compulsion as the primary route through which free riding can be avoided. This is debatable; people comply with social preferences for the most part through socialization and the establishment of social norms (▶ I.1.c), and compulsion usually plays a limited part. It is undeniable, though, that there comes a point at which compulsion may be introduced.

The argument for compelling free riders applies only to part of the argument for collective action. It does not apply to mutual aid, because someone who does not contribute to a mutual aid society does not benefit, and it does not apply to national welfare systems which have been based on that principle. Free riding is a problem only when the action cannot exclude recipients. This mainly applies to action for the provision of universal benefits – benefits and services which are available to everyone – and to public goods or services, like roads, street lighting, parks, policing and defence.

The argument for compulsion is straightforward enough. If I use a service which I have not paid for, I am liable in civil law for an action by the owners. If the owners are the rest of the community, the principle is no different; I have no evident right to use their services without con-tributing. But there are two special cases which need to be considered. One is the case of goods which free riders will benefit from whether or not they pay. Public health and street lighting affect everyone, whether

---

91 D. Stone (1997) *Policy paradox*, 2nd edition, New York: Norton, pp. 220–221.

or not they want to be a part of it. The main case for compulsion here is that people are benefiting. But there is also an argument about 'externality'; the effects of such goods are not felt exclusively by one person, but spin off throughout society. Without a road network, transport becomes difficult; without transport, the distribution of goods and services fails; without the distribution of services, choices are limited. The interdependence of people in society makes inclusion in certain activities unavoidable.[92]

The second case, which is much more problematic, is where services are divisible, and people choose not to participate in a collective service because they prefer not to use it. This can be dismissed in some cases, like education, defence or health care, because people benefit as members of a society. They benefit because others use the service: other people's education makes technology possible, and other people's health protects our health. But there are other cases, like parks or libraries, where people might genuinely not use the service. The difficulty of admitting this point is that parks and sewer networks do not flourish in economic markets, and without the elements of compulsion and inclusion, they probably would not exist. (The point is acknowledged by Adam Smith in *The wealth of nations*.)[93] The main argument for such compulsion seems to be that a society can legitimately make rules for the general benefit of its members; the economic argument can be made that the benefit to each member of the population outweighs the social cost. The test is then whether such restrictions can be justified in terms of the freedom of individuals. This argument is probably not sufficient to override the objections of liberals, because it denies individual choice; but it would be satisfactory to those who believe that society should be organized for the convenience and comfort of its members.

I.3.b.iii(2)   Collective action does not have to be compulsory.

Some degree of compulsion is defensible. Any argument that collective action must depend on compulsion, however, would be mistaken.[94] It would be mistaken both in theory, for the reasons which are outlined here, and in fact: many arrangements for mutual aid, and the foundation of several welfare states have been made on a voluntary basis. For example, until very recently there was no direct requirement to join the systems which protected people from unemployment and sickness in Denmark, Sweden and Finland. Compulsion was considered unnecessary, because there was no scope for free riding and the benefits of

---

92 W. Oakland (1987) 'Theory of public goods', ch. 9 of A. Auerbach and M. Feldstein, *Handbook of public economics*, vol. 2, Amsterdam: North Holland.

93 Smith (1776), Book 4, ch. IX.

94 Here I part company from de Swaan: see de Swaan (1988), pp. 159–160.

joining were clear. (Compulsory contributions were finally introduced as a means of raising revenue to cope with the economic downturn of the 1990s – in other words, as a form of taxation.)[95] Collective action may be compulsory, then, but it does not have to be. Because compulsion is not requisite, it is not a key element in the theoretical analysis presented here; it will be referred to later in the contexts where it occurs.

I.3.b.iv   Collective action and mutual aid develop spontaneously in society.

People live in society (▸ I.1.a); society is formed of groups (▸ I.2.b); and where there are social groups, people act collectively (▸ I.2.a.iv). This form of collective action is reinforced both by moral considerations (▸ I.3.a.iii) and by rational self-interest (▸ I.3.b). This is especially important for an understanding of the provision of welfare, which this book is about. Historically, collective action and mutual aid are the origin of many arrangements for the provision of welfare in Europe and America; social protection was developed through the actions of occupational groups, guilds, fraternities and mutual aid societies.[96] Although such action developed through civil society, it is often seen in the present day as the product of state action. This is reflected in the competing historical accounts referred to at the outset of the argument (▸ Method). The emphasis on the state has arisen because many states sought subsequently either to direct or to supplant the role of collective action in provision; but we must not disregard the importance of the collective action which generally precedes state action. Some form of collective action is typical of any society – indeed, it comes close to defining what a society is. It appears to be 'spontaneous' because formal decision-making and the intervention of governments are not necessary for it to happen.

Cohesion and exclusion

I.3.c   Solidarity is an integral aspect of social cohesion.

The principle of solidarity is rationally based and morally desirable, but neither of these features fully explains its force. Solidarity is identified

---

95 N. Ploug and J. Kvist (eds) (1994) *Recent trends in cash benefits in Europe*, Copenhagen: Danish National Institute of Social Research.

96 P. Baldwin (1990) *The politics of social solidarity*, Cambridge: Cambridge University Press; D. Beito (1997) '"This enormous army": the mutual aid tradition of American fraternal societies before the twentieth century', in E. Paul, F. Miller and J. Paul (eds) *The welfare state*, Cambridge: Cambridge University Press.

with the obligations which people have towards others within a society. Because people in any society are liable to be interdependent to some degree, and interdependence implies obligation, there is probably no form of society in which some form of solidarity does not apply. If society is an interwoven series of networks (▶ I.2.b), solidaristic obligations are often the threads which bind the networks together. This is another way of describing social cohesion (▶ I.2.b.i). Solidarity is not the only process through which social cohesion might be developed – culture, belief or common interest matter just as much – but it is integral to social cohesion, and wherever there is a degree of social cohesion, some elements of solidarity are likely to be found. Solidarity is integral to social cohesion. The same can be said of its relationship to society, because without social cohesion, societies cannot exist.

I.3.c.i   Collective action defines a community.

Collective action is action undertaken by a social group (▶ I.2.a.iv). Although identity is one of the characteristics of groups, it is not always very strong. Some collective organizations are strictly formal; the members of a friendly society or insurees of a mutual insurance company may think of themselves as customers rather than participants, and respond to contact with the society as if they were dealing with a commercial undertaking. However, collective action often has the effect of building group identity, either because it formalizes links and relationships which were already evident – like church societies, miners' welfare groups, or parent-teacher associations – or because it defines the group in relation to the wider society. When, for example, Afro-Caribbean societies have been formed in English cities, they have been identified as a focus and voice for a community. The links between people from different parts of the Caribbean and Africa were often tenuous at first, but the combination of social contact within the group and the perception of the wider society has helped to forge a group identity.

One of the vaguest forms of social group, though one which has been profoundly influential in social policy, is the 'community'. Communities can be formed through physical identification: a household, a village or a city might be seen as a group. There may be some common characteristic or feature which links the members; a group can consist of elderly people in an area, or a business community. The term is also used to refer to people who are engaged in some common activity: there may be a 'community' of business people, politicians or journalists. It is not very clear what makes people into a 'community' – Hillery, in an article written in the 1950s, identified 94 distinct meanings of the term[97] – but

---

97 G. Hillery (1955) 'Definitions of community: areas of agreement', *Rural Sociology*, 20: 111–123.

generally it implies that there is something about the members of the community that means they can be taken to form a group of some kind. Because collective action defines a group, it also defines a community.

I.3.c.ii Collective action is exclusive as well as inclusive.

The process of forming and defining groups has a double edge. On one hand, it serves to focus, and sometimes to accentuate, relationships within the group. On the other, it defines a social border – the relationship of the group to the people outside it. Social borders vary in strength and permeability, but their importance is difficult to overstate. It seems to be a general trend that social groups develop their identity either by reinforcing contact within the group or by strengthening the limits.

Social groups tend, as a result, to be exclusive as well as inclusive. The very act of inclusion implies social borders, because the more clearly a group is defined, the more clearly insiders and outsiders can be identified. The most extreme example of such borders occurs in a caste society, where strict rules are used to identify the boundaries between castes.[98] Crossing boundaries is defined as an act of 'pollution', and so a basic form of deviance. In modern societies, borders are less strongly identified, but there is still a strong residual element of these rules in the stigmatization of deviant groups, including poor, mentally disordered and disabled people.[99]

The process of defining borders does not mean that obligations to people cease to exist altogether. On the same argument which implies obligations to people across social divisions (▶ I.2.c.iii), there are residual obligations to people who are within the same society. These obligations are generally seen, however, as inferior to duties to people who are members of the same social group. Solidarity and social cohesion may coexist with structures of disadvantage and social division (▶ I.2.c.ii).

I.3.c.iii Exclusion prevents social integration.

Exclusion refers, in this context, to two closely related but distinct problems. First, there are people who fall outside the borders of social groups – people who are stigmatized and socially rejected. There is a long history of the social and physical isolation of certain groups, such as

---

98 M. Douglas (1966) *Purity and danger*, London: Routledge and Kegan Paul.
99 P. Spicker (1984) *Stigma and social welfare*, Beckenham: Croom Helm.

people with disabilities, who are regarded as deviant.[100] Second, there are those who are not part of solidaristic social networks, experiencing neither obligations to others nor support from them. The extreme case is that of the single homeless person, living on the street, with no family contact. There are degrees of exclusion, however; as the number and strength of relationships diminish, it is difficult to define any single point at which a person can be said to be 'excluded'. A pensioner who is afraid to leave her house, a single parent on an outlying estate who does not have enough money to travel into town to shop, an unemployed man who has little hope of returning to work, or the residents of a nursing home, might be said to be 'excluded' to some degree, but the degree varies; all can be expected to retain at least some contact with family, friends and the activities of the wider society.

Exclusion is, then, a function of social integration, and it varies directly with the degree of integration a person has. But it is also an obstacle to social integration, because exclusion diminishes the ability of people to participate in society. If people do not have social contact, they do not form the relationships, or become part of a network of obligations, to the same extent as others. Those who are highly integrated become better integrated still; those who are less integrated are marginalized.

I.3.c.iv   Exclusion limits social cohesion.

Exclusion has, too, a wider social implication, beyond its implications for the person. The effect of exclusion on the wider society is to distinguish an in-group – those who are protected and supported by networks of social relationships and solidarity – from those who are not. Arguably this strengthens the in-group,[101] but cohesion is a product of the strength of relationships within the group, not of the borders (▸ I.2.b.i). However, when exclusion is widespread, the security and well-being of those who are included are also jeopardized. Exclusion diminishes the strength, not only of the obligation to the excluded, but of the obligations which the excluded have to others. Exclusion is often associated, perhaps unfairly, with a sense of social threat. Part of this is generated by uncertainty: where there are large numbers of people who have few obligations

---

100 J. Hanks and L. Hanks (1948) 'The physically handicapped in certain non-occidental societies', *Journal of Social Issues*, 4 (4): 11–20; P. Hunt (ed.) (1966) *Stigma*, London: Chapman; M. Jacques (1960) 'Treatment of the disabled in primitive cultures', in C. Patterson (ed.) *Readings in rehabilitation counselling*, Champaign, IL: Stipes Publishing; M. Oliver (1990) *The politics of disablement*, London: Macmillan.

101 R. Scott (1972) 'A proposed framework for analysing deviance as a property of social order', in R. Scott and J. Douglas, *Theoretical perspectives on deviance*, New York: Basic Books.

towards others in society, and little interaction, it is difficult to know how they will react or what can be expected of them. Exclusion generates insecurity.

From the perspective of the whole society, then, exclusion has the effect of reducing cohesion. It does this by alienating those who are excluded so that they have fewer responsibilities towards others in society, and others have fewer responsibilities towards them; by generating insecurity even among those who are included; and, from the perspective of the whole society, by reducing the strength of the obligations to those who are relatively distant, and so to strangers. The Single European Act of 1987, on this basis, made provision in the European Community for the promotion of 'economic and social cohesion'. The principal measure undertaken under this heading has been the reform of the Structural Funds, which are described as 'instruments for combatting the exclusion from the labour market of the weakest sections of the population'.[102]

Social responsibility and social borders

I.3.d   Obligations may extend beyond borders.

The processes which link social groups (▶ I.2.a.iii) cut across social divisions and geographical boundaries. The links across social divisions are necessary for the continuance of a society (▶ I.2.c.iii). The links which extend beyond geographical boundaries, to different societies, are not so immediately obvious. Contemporary societies are interdependent. Proximity, interaction and exchange lead, not just to increasing contact, but to the development of a complex set of networks, involving mutual obligation, interdependence and shared codes. This process is clearest in the case of the economy, where the process of exchange has led to greater interdependence; but the same trends are visible in culture and social interaction.

The general name which has been given to this trend is 'globalization'. The term is something of a misnomer, because it underestimates the degree of remoteness, and the tenuousness of social contact, between different parts of the world; the principal international relationships fall into definable trading blocs,[103] and the contact which takes place beyond those blocs is relatively limited. Interdependence may also take the form of structural dependency, in which some countries are relegated to a

---

102 European Commission (1994) *EC Structural Funds 4th Report: the implementation of the reform of the Structural Funds*, Brussels: Commission of the European Communities, p. 25.

103 P. Hirst and G. Thompson (1996) *Globalisation in question*, Cambridge: Polity.

subordinate, and potentially an exploited, role in the world economy.[104] But it is clear, in either case, that relationships do not stop within the confines of any particular society. If relationships continue beyond borders, so do moral obligations.

I.3.d.i Solidarity is local and national.

The relationships of solidarity which people have diminish in strength with social distance (▶ I.3.a.i) – it is virtually a definition of what social distance is. For many people, if not most, these relationships follow defined geographical patterns. The organization of solidarity remains, for many, determinedly local. It is bound, through the neighbourhood, city and region, to a particular place and time. These patterns are partly defined by nationality.

It has been argued, by Elie Kedourie, that there is no substance in the idea of the nation, which in historical terms is a fairly recent development.[105] It is generally true in sociology that the things which people believe are liable to be true in their consequences, and even if nationality is not based in any firm, objective truth, nationhood plays a major part in the formation of social policy. Language and culture are key elements in formal socialization, particularly in schools. A sense of nationality tends to follow from this, sometimes supporting, and sometimes frustrating, the attempts of nationalists to preserve historical, cultural and linguistic identity. It also determines legal status, which can affect where people can move and where they can work. The impact of nationality on contact, status and the structure of obligation tends to identify solidarity closely with national identity. Nationality defines the nation as the root of a solidaristic community. This may put the matter too high; it is also possible to see national solidarity, as in France, as an agglomeration of local solidarities, and as such a more distant, less powerful source of responsibility.

I.3.d.ii Social responsibility is not confined to national boundaries.

This begs the question whether it is possible to develop solidarity across national boundaries. People feel differently towards strangers in other countries than they do to strangers in their own, and this remains true even if they are likely to have social contact with those strangers. Despite the European Union, there is little fellow feeling evident between, say,

---

104 S.A. Samad (1996) 'The present situation in poverty research', in E. Øyen, S. Miller and S.A. Samad (eds) *Poverty: a global review*, Oslo: Scandinavian University Press, pp. 33–46.
105 E. Kedourie (1993) *Nationalism*, Oxford: Blackwell.

France and Austria, and French citizens are more likely to acknowledge responsibility for someone from New Caledonia (legally a part of France) than they are to acknowledge responsibility for an Austrian.

This example helps to clarify something of the nature of solidarity, and of social proximity. Social proximity is not the same as geographical proximity; networks of solidarity develop through common history, contacts, interaction, trade, military conquest and so forth. Britain is closer to South Africa or India than it is to Albania. In some cases, the interaction is regional and geographically based: the US is bound, willy-nilly, to Mexico. Some of the ties are through common religious and linguistic links, as with the Arab countries of the Middle East, or the continued links between Spain and Latin America. Because interaction and interdependence extend beyond national boundaries, the same is true of solidarity.

I.4

THE MORAL COMMUNITY

I.4 People and communities have to act morally.

Moral rules
  I.4.a   *People are bound by moral rules.*
  I.4.a.i   Moral ideas form rules of action.
  I.4.a.ii   Moral rules are social norms.

The social construction of morality
  I.4.b   *Moral rules are socially constructed.*
  I.4.b.i   Moral norms are complex, and sometimes
              contradictory.
  I.4.b.ii   The morality of an action cannot be judged by its
              consequences.
  I.4.b.iii   Morality is not rational.

Deviance and control
  I.4.c   *Morals justify intervention in other people's lives.*
  I.4.c.i   Societies control undesirable behaviour.
  I.4.c.ii   Deviance is a breach of social rules.
  I.4.c.iii   Deviance implies exclusion.

Moral approaches to social action
  I.4.d   *Where there are social relationships, there are moral*
              relationships.
  I.4.d.i   Morals govern personal and social life.
  I.4.d.ii   The morality of collective action depends on the nature of
              the action.

The moral community
  I.4.e   *Societies also have moral obligations.*
  I.4.e.i   Societies have obligations to their members.
  I.4.e.ii   Societies have obligations to non-members.
  I.4.e.iii   Societies have obligations to other societies.

I.4.e.iv   Societies have obligations to previous generations.
I.4.e.v   Societies have obligations to future generations.
I.4.e.vi   Societies can be moral agents.

Moral rules

I.4.a   People are bound by moral rules.

People are moral agents. They have responsibilities to other people
(▶ I.3.a.ii). Moral norms require them to act in particular ways; they are
expected to behave according to certain standards, and they may be
subject to a social sanction if they do not. The application of moral rules
usually depends on there being a reason for a person's action; morals are
the codes which are used to determine whether an action is acceptable.
In the criminal law, a criminal act requires two constituent elements: the
mens rea, or guilty mind, and the *actus reus*, or guilty act. An action
which is involuntary or accidental is not likely to be criminal (though
there are exceptions, of strict liability); an action which is not itself
unlawful is not usually criminal, even if the consequences are bad.[106]
Much the same is true of morality: actions are judged by their nature,
not by their consequences.

The suggestion that people 'have to' act morally does not mean that
they can only act morally; they have to act morally because they are
obliged to do so by their moral code. If they do not act morally, they are
in breach of the rules.

I.4.a.i   Moral ideas form rules of action.

Morals are rules governing behaviour. Rules can define the limits of
acceptable action, and they can identify desirable action; many moral
rules do both. 'Thou shalt not kill' is the first kind of rule; 'honour thy
father and thy mother' is the second. The first type is easier to enforce
than the second, because it is easier to tell when it has not been followed.
Prohibitions tend, as a result, to be more prominent in discussions of
morality than virtues.[107]

This tends to distance the discussion of morality from the discussion of
social norms in other senses. Social norms are expectations (▶ I.1.c).
Morals, however, are often defined by contrast with expectations, rather
than by conformity with them. They may be concerned with what people
are expected not to do. Because of this, the nature of moral conduct is

---

106 J. Smith and B. Hogan (1996) *Criminal law*, 8th edition, London: Butterworth.
107 Contrast the position in D. Statman (ed.) (1997) *Virtue ethics: a critical
reader*, Edinburgh: Edinburgh University Press.

concealed from view. We do not think of people as acting 'morally' just because they talk to each other rather than hitting each other, walk past houses without stealing from them, or pay for goods in shops. But we would know immediately that they were not acting morally if they did otherwise.

This does not mean that moral rules do not apply in such cases. However, such rules are so strong, and so evident, that there is little reason to explain or justify them; they are an everyday part of social life.

I.4.a.ii Moral rules are social norms.

Moral concepts convey expectations about the ways in which people should behave; they are, then, a form of social norm (► I.1.c). They are different from other social norms in three main respects. First, they are rules, which are subject to social sanctions (and so, which are enforceable). This does not mean that there has to be a formal sanction, though often there will be; social disapproval and rejection are also sanctions for immorality. Second, they are rules about behaviour. Many of the social expectations we have are not concerned with behaviour or conduct. They relate to physical appearance, personality, social roles and status – in other words, to any aspect of individual and social relationships. Moral rules have a more limited focus; they are concerned primarily with actions. (It should be acknowledged, at the same time, that this coexists with an older form of morality, which ascribes behaviour to people on the basis of their lineage. People can be stigmatized morally because of what their parents or ancestors did.) Third, moral rules are serious. Issues which are not thought of as important are either not subject to a sanction, or reduced to matters of etiquette.

The identification of moral values with social norms means that, like other social norms, they depend on the society they are found in. They are not subjective, and they are not individual. They are based, rather, on shared, intersubjective perceptions, developed through the process of socialization, and disseminated through social interaction (► I.1.c).

The view of morality this offers is different from that found in moral philosophy. Moral philosophies – such as Kantianism, utilitarianism or virtue ethics – have generally sought the foundation of morality in its own internal rationale. The argument here, by contrast, is a sociological one: moral rules are a category of social norms, derived and held through a similar process to other social norms.

The social construction of morality

I.4.b Moral rules are socially constructed.

The idea that morality is 'socially constructed' does not mean that it is artificial or imposed; it means that the concepts which are used, and the relationships between them, are developed in social terms. The processes by which moral norms are established are complex. Some moral codes emerge through 'prescription'. Actions which are done repeatedly with beneficial effects condition expectations, and expectations generate norms (▶ I.1.c). Over time, rules become established in society.[108] Rules against murder, theft and public disorder exist because these acts threaten the security of everyone, and a society is better off without them.

Morality is not fixed; the process of prescription depends on the assumption that there are other processes which are being introduced, tried and either rejected or retained. Some moral principles appear to be relatively recent, like the tolerance of suicide in Western countries or the reaction against the corporal punishment of children, though often recent changes simply reflect the adaptation of existing norms to new circumstances. Rules can be imported from other societies, through 'cultural diffusion'. On the grand scale, the growth of Christianity is illustrative; more recently, the cultural dominance of the United States means that many people have sought to incorporate the liberal individualism of the US within their own culture, sometimes with paradoxical results. Rules can be imposed by law, and the moral authority which supports the law invests those rules with a sense of legitimacy. If, for example, the law says that young people should not buy alcohol, it will immediately become immoral to break that rule – because it is immoral to break the law – and that sense of immorality will be shared by people who have no particular feelings about the morality of alcohol consumption. (This creates a dilemma, and so a tension, for those who feel that certain laws are unjust and should be disobeyed.) This also provides a route through which some moral principles can be consciously introduced by legislators, and educational courses in religious instruction or civic responsibility have been used to foster particular moral views.

I.4.b.i Moral norms are complex, and sometimes contradictory.

Moral rules relate to the way in which people live their lives, and the way that people live their lives is rarely straightforward. A single act can have many different implications, and be subject to many rules at the same time. Moral dilemmas – points at which moral rules conflict – are common. The values of work and family lead to conflicting demands on time and commitment: single parents are condemned both for going out to work and for staying at home. Parents whose children commit criminal offences are torn between moral condemnation of the offence and the moral imperative to stand by their child.

---

108 E. Burke (1790) *Reflections on the revolution in France*, New York: Holt, Rinehart and Winston, 1959.

The example of abortion stands out; it is difficult to think of a case in which the moral dilemmas are so sharply defined. The termination of a pregnancy is subject not to one moral norm, but to several, relating to the unborn child, the mother, the father, other involved people, women in general, and the wider society. Although some of the protagonists in the debate present one, and only one of these positions, most people would recognize the legitimacy of more than one. This is why the issue is so complex and difficult, because the interests and positions of those involved are hard to balance, and may be irreconcilable.

I.4.b.ii   The morality of an action cannot be judged by its consequences.

Morality is generally concerned with what is right, not just with what has a good effect. There are, certainly, many cases where it will be right to have a good effect, and there are some moral principles which value an action according to the consequences. Some people do argue that whether or not something has good consequences is at the root of morality; this is the basis of utilitarianism.[109] There are two forms of utilitarianism. Act-utilitarianism argues that right actions are simply those with good results. By that argument, it is all right to kill someone who makes everyone around them miserable, like the victim in an Agatha Christie novel or university Heads of Department, and it is all right to rob a bank if the money wouldn't have been spent otherwise, because spending the money increases employment and the sum of happiness. This is unlikely to persuade many people over the moral age of seven, and it can be fairly rapidly dismissed. The alternative doctrine, rule-utilitarianism, argues that a rule is morally right if it is likely to have good effects when practised generally. As a moral doctrine, this is still questionable. Locking up people whose innocence is in doubt might be justified by the consequences, but most modern societies do not accept that it is fair to the person who is locked up. All this means that actions can be thought to be morally right even when they do not have good consequences. Although they are linked, the two ideas are discrete – that is, logically separable – and distinct in practice.

Whether a moral action has undesirable consequences depends, of course, on one's view of whether the action is actually moral, and whether the actions are actually undesirable. A cloying, cloistering morality – the kind which was used to repress a caste society – could seem highly beneficial to some, including many of its victims, while deeply objectionable to others, including some of its beneficiaries. But there are cases where 'moral' actions have had clearly undesirable

---

109 J.S. Mill (1861) 'Utilitarianism', in M. Warnock (ed.) Utilitarianism, Glasgow: Collins, 1962.

consequences: for example, the prohibition of alcohol in the US (which fostered gangsterism, corruption and law-breaking), or the maintenance of property rights during the Irish famine, which led to food being exported in the sight of people who were starving.[110]

Conversely, actions with desirable consequences can be immoral. Breaking promises is wrong, even if the promise should not have been made. Many things in life are enjoyable, pleasant and morally disapproved; as an old song says, if it feels good, it's probably illegal, immoral or it makes you fat. The problem here is that in real life moral principles often conflict, and things which are desirable for one reason may be undesirable for another.

I.4.b.iii Morality is not rational.

Some philosophical systems have attempted to describe morality in rational terms, identifying moral codes with consistent general principles. Utilitarianism is one such system; the most important of the others Kantian thought and contractarianism. Kantian approaches begin from general, universal propositions about morality which can in principle be applied to everyone.[111] Contractarianism rests on an explanatory myth, trying to identify what reasonable people might agree to if they make their decisions under a 'veil of ignorance' as to the actual consequences.[112]

The central flaw of any rational system is the presupposition that existing morality can be said to comply, more or less, with its precepts. Rational approaches to morality are presented as both a form of moral teaching and a description of the way in which morals work. There may well be moral codes which fail to comply with the theory, but these are liable to be dismissed as aberrations. If moral norms appear to be out of step with the ideal moral principles, the flaw rests in the norms, not in the principles. Most systems of thought are subject to two closely related intellectual vices. The first is the assumption that the morality which the writer holds is a dictate of reason, rather than a social construct. The trend is visible, in different ways, in John Stuart Mill's defence of the utility of tolerance[113] and John Rawls's extraordinary assumption that the values of liberal America are the values to which every rational person must assent.[114] The second is the inability of rationalist explanations to accommodate changes in morality when the

---

110 J. Drèze and A. Sen (1989) *Hunger and public action*, Oxford: Clarendon Press.

111 H. Paton (1965) *The moral law*, London: Hutchinson.

112 J. Rawls (1971) *A theory of justice*, Oxford: Oxford University Press.

113 Mill (1861).

114 Rawls (1971); and see N. Daniels (ed.) (1975) *Reading Rawls*, Oxford: Blackwell.

differences have no evident function. It seems fairly obvious that sexual mores differ strikingly between societies, and sometimes differ within a short space of time in the same society; a rational, universal, consistent code cannot begin to cope with this. The truth is that these moral codes depend on the society they are part of, and they are not susceptible to rational analysis.

The attraction of rational explanations is that they are so often nearly right. Moral principles often fall tantalizingly near to rational outcomes. Axelrod's model of the evolution of co-operation shows that for rational actors faced with choices about co-operation or defection the best strategy for survival is 'tit for tat' – returning good for good, and evil for evil.[115] Over time, social mores seem to conform to rational principles.

The explanation for this is that morality evolves, like many other social processes, through a process of selection. The idea of prescription seems to imply a functional view of morality: moral precepts are retained if they work. But the same process leads to some irrational outcomes. Moral codes can be retained long after they have ceased to be beneficial. (The law of rape is an illustration: conceived primarily as a means of protecting men's property rights in women, the law of rape remains the principal protection for women against sexual abuse by men. But there are sexual assaults against women which are far more serious than rape, whether that is assessed in moral terms, by the harm done, or by the degradation of the woman; conversely, there are rapes in which the element of abuse or exploitation is relatively marginal.) It is also possible that a rule might become established which has a very negative effect: for centuries, women's abilities have been disregarded because of a stereo-typical view of their role.

Deviance and control

I.4.c Morals justify intervention in other people's lives.

The rules of action implied by morals apply to everyone in a society; often, in the view of people in that society, they apply to everyone outside it. Since the Enlightenment, there has been a tendency for indi-vidualists to treat morality as a personal matter, and some reluctance to impose moral codes on other people. The kinds of moral issue about which this is true are limited to a few important areas, such as religious worship, and even then there are substantial qualifications to make. People are not free to do what they please, and even the most fervent individualists generally accept that there should be some restrictions, most typically when actions begin to affect other people.

---

115 G. Axelrod (1990) *The evolution of co-operation*, Harmondsworth: Penguin.

J.S. Mill wrote that the individual

> cannot rightfully be compelled to do or forbear because it will be better for him to do so, because it will make him happier, because, in the opinion of others, to do so would be wise, or even right. These may be good reasons for remonstrating with him, or reasoning with him, or persuading him, or entreating him, but not for compelling him, or visiting him with any evil in case he do otherwise. To justify that, the conduct from which it is desired to deter him must be calculated to produce evil to some one else.[116]

This is not a limitation which is reflected in common morality. If moral codes are right, they are usually thought to be right for other people as well, and most people apply moral restrictions to the actions of others, whether or not third parties are affected. Moral disapproval of dangerous drugs was evident long before they were actually banned, and very few people (the exceptions are 'libertarians' in the United States) seriously advocate legalization currently. Equally, there are positive rules which people consider that others ought to accept. This is one of the rationales for the virus of religious evangelism.

Intervention in other people's lives is sometimes described as 'paternalistic'. This is a derogatory term, at least in the West, because there is the implication that intervention is treating people like children. So, for example, a recent paper from the British government on the situation of people with severe dementia shies away from the idea of intervention to protect vulnerable old people from abuse and exploitation because this will 'infantilize' them.[117] This misunderstands the position of children and adults both. Children need protection because they are vulnerable, not because they are inferior. Adults may also need protection in certain circumstances, and whether or not children might also have such protection is an irrelevance; what matters is the situation of the adult.

I.4.c.i *Societies control undesirable behaviour.*

Norms, and moral rules, combine expectations with sanctions (▶ I.1.c; I.4.a.ii), and there are strong social responses to inadmissable behaviour. On one hand, there are positive moral codes, expressing approval and offering rewards for approved behaviour; on the other there are prohibitions, expressing disapproval and imposing stigmatization or punishment. Part of the socialization of children is concerned with enabling children not just to recognize the rules, but to internalize them: to accept the rules, and to behave in conformity with moral principles 'naturally', without even having to think about them. Those who do not internalize

---

116 J.S. Mill (1859) 'On liberty', in M. Warnock (ed.) *Utilitarianism*, Glasgow: Collins (1962), p. 135.

117 Lord Chancellor's Department (1997) *Who decides?* London: HMSO.

the rules – and many do not – are subject to external sanction. Ruth Benedict once made a helpful distinction between 'guilt' and 'shame' cultures.[118] A 'guilt' culture is one in which norms are internalized and accepted; the main constraint on immoral action is the guilt people feel. A 'shame' culture is one which relies on external sanction; the main constraint is the fear of being caught, and public exposure. (The effect of punishment is, of course, to emphasize shame rather than guilt; this is why physical punishment, like corporal punishment of children, is generally ineffective in instilling moral values. In so far as it externalizes the sanction, it is likely to have the reverse of the desired effect.)

The control of unacceptable behaviour is not, then, just a matter of punishment or stigmatization. It begins in the earliest stages of a person's life; it is part of the process of socialization. People who subsequently deviate are liable, not just to punishment, but to various steps which might re-educate, or reintegrate, them, into the pattern of conduct approved by society. I mentioned previously the curious condition of psychopathy, in which people appear to be under-socialized and unable to accept social responsibilities to each other. The response to psychopathy is not nominally to punish psychopaths (though psychopaths can be detained if they are a danger to others), but to treat them for their condition – despite the fact that psychopathy is not, technically speaking, a mental illness. The effectiveness of treatment is uncertain, but the better results appear to come from treatments which focus on social behaviour.[119]

I.4.c.ii Deviance is a breach of social rules.

The term which social scientists use for a breach of social rules is 'deviance'. The opposite of deviance is 'normality' – that is, conformity with norms.

Deviance is a wider concept than immoral action, because there are many other kinds of expectation. For example, people can be 'physically deviant', if they are different enough to breach expectations,[120] and (however perversely) they can be subjected to the same kinds of sanction as people who are in breach of moral rules.[121]

People, and not just actions, can be considered deviant. The general principle of criminal law in modern societies is that people are tried for

118 R. Benedict (1946) *The chrysanthemum and the sword*, Boston, MA: Houghton Mifflin.

119 M. Gelder et al. (1989) *Oxford textbook of psychiatry*, 2nd edition, Oxford: Oxford University Press, ch. 5.

120 R.J. Comer and J.A. Piliavin (1972) 'The effects of physical deviance upon face-to-face interaction: the other side', in D. Boswell and J. Wingrove (eds), *The handicapped person in the community*, London: Tavistock, 1974.

121 P. Spicker (1984) *Stigma and social welfare*, Beckenham: Croom Helm.

what they have done, not for what they are:[122] but social norms often reject people for what they are, not for what they have done. This leads to the strange position where someone can do something in breach of social norms without 'being' deviant, while someone else might act in conformity with the rules and yet still be stigmatized.

I.4.c.iii   Deviance implies exclusion.

The principal sanction used against people who are deviant is social exclusion – rejecting them, cutting them off from social contact, and denying obligations towards them. This is not, of course, the only possible reaction: some traditional societies have emphasized the reverse, which is the reintegration of the deviant person into the community.[123]

The process of rejection is also referred to as 'stigmatization', though a 'stigma' might also refer to a label attached to the condition which is disapproved. The effect of stigmatization is to send a clear signal, both to the person who is deviant and to others, that deviance is unacceptable; in principle, it should be possible for the stigmatized person to be reintegrated, but to do this the person should wish to co-operate, and there is no reason to do this if the condition is not in some way undesirable. Stigma is often, however, used unproductively. If the condition is already undesirable – like poverty, unemployment or physical impairment – the motivation of stigmatized people is unlikely to be stirred further by the process of stigmatization, and the effect of social rejection may be to obstruct reintegration. There is then potentially a contradiction between stigma and exclusion, on the one hand, and the desire to treat or reintegrate deviants on the other.

Moral approaches to social action

I.4.d   Where there are social relationships, there are moral relationships.

Wherever there are social relationships, there are moral relationships. Social relationships generate expectations, and expectations underlie morality (▶ I.1.c; I.4.a.ii); but this is only part of the story. Moral relationships are not only generated by social relationships; they are also preconditions for them. Without a minimal degree of security, interaction with strangers becomes dangerous or impossible. There are, then, rules which govern people before their first encounter, as well as expectations which develop in the course of a relationship.

---

122 But see F. Neumann (1942) *Behemoth*, London: Gollancz.

123 S. Nadel (1953) 'Social control and self-regulation', *Social Forces*, 31 (3): 265–273.

This does not mean that every social relationship is also a moral relationship. It means, rather, that every social relationship is governed by moral principles. Some of these principles are negative prohibitions, like respect for people's bodies and private space, and they become visible only when they are breached. Some are positive, like the duty to reciprocate for things received; but that duty is initially weak, and becomes stronger as interaction and relationships of exchange develop.

I.4.d.i Morals govern personal and social life.

Morality has no evident limits, and that has troubled many commentators who believe that there should be parts of life which are unregulated. If morality is based on expectations, it does not seem to matter that the expectations are unreasonable, intrusive or oppressive. Some religious codes have prescriptions for almost every part of a person's waking life (as well as some of the times when people are asleep).

This position can only effectively be opposed by an alternative moral position, and that is what liberals do. They argue, not that there are no moral rules which apply at the level of the individual person, but that the value of individual liberty overrides them. This leaves the question of valuation. Charles Taylor makes the argument, persuasively, that the value of liberty depends on the value of the activity which we are free to pursue. Freedom of religion, freedom of assembly or freedom of speech matter a great deal; the freedom to drive a car without using the brakes does not, and no one seriously thinks that traffic lights are a major infringement on liberty.[124] But debates about freedom can still be triggered by fairly minor issues, precisely because the value of what is being limited – the power to act without interference – is greater than the justification for the infringement.

The same arguments apply, *a fortiori*, to social relationships. Morals may limit the scope for certain types of social action; the central issue is whether or not they outweigh other principles governing social interaction.

I.4.d.ii The morality of collective action depends on the nature of the action.

Collective action is action by a group (▶ I.2.a.iv), and it can refer to a wide range of different activities. Like any other form of social relationship, collective action is subject to moral rules. The rules concerning collective action, like many other moral rules, depend on whether the action is

---

124 C. Taylor (1979) 'What's wrong with negative liberty?' in A. Ryan (ed.) *The idea of freedom*, Oxford: Oxford University Press.

itself acceptable. Conspiracies and gangs are unacceptable when their objects are unacceptable. (The term 'conspiracy' is of course pejorative, because people who band together for an acceptable purpose, like arranging a garden festival, are not thought of as conspirators.) There is nothing self-evidently moral about much group activity, because activity which is not in breach of norms is an accepted part of everyday life. Forming a discussion group, celebrating a birth or watching a sports match are neither moral nor immoral in themselves; there is a pre-sumption that these are acceptable activities, and moral concerns are raised only if there is some reason to think otherwise.

Collective action, like any other kind of social relationship, depends on certain preconditions. The preconditions are not the same as those for casual interaction, because collective action concerns groups, and groups have a common identity; people do not make families, associations or communities on the basis of casual contact, but through patterns of established relationships. This makes it difficult to generalize about groups, because the morality of group formation depends strongly on a pre-defined context.

The moral community

I.4.e Societies also have moral obligations.

A society is a meta-group: it embraces and subsumes the identity of the groups within it (► I.2.b). If a group can have obligations (► I.2.a.iii), so can a society.

I.4.e.i Societies have obligations to their members.

Any social group can have relationships with its members, and societies are no different; there is no great difficulty about the proposition that a society can have obligations to its members. A 'society' is a large, shifting mass of relationships, but it is also a group; as such, it stands for the generality of persons within it. Any obligation which is owed to people in general is owed to that society. Conversely, any obligations which are held in general towards people – and so, any claim rights they may have – are held by the society they are in.

I.4.e.ii Societies have obligations to non-members.

More problematic is the position of people who are not members of a society: for example people in transit through a country. If they have obligations to the society they are found in, they are not very clear ones. There does seem to be a general expectation that tourists and visitors will respect the customs and laws of a country.

For the most part, non-members of society are assumed to be members of another society. (The case of stateless persons is exceptional. If someone is not part of any society, it has been accepted that the place where that person happens to be is the place which should take them in. At that point, the stateless person is effectively admitted to membership of the society – on a purely formal basis, because the stateless person may have no social contact or relationship with the society he or she is seeking to join.)

If people are assumed to be members of another society, it would seem to follow that their relationship with the host society should depend on the relationship between the two societies. This is not consistently the case. For example, a German citizen has virtually free access to Britain, with reciprocal rights relating to the provision of health care; an Afghani does not. But a German citizen who commits a criminal offence would, like the Afghani, be subject to exclusion or deportation. This is best explained in two stages. First, there are general duties which apply to the non-members of a society. Non-members are generally subject to the law of a host country. Second, there may be specific additional duties to members of another society, depending on the relationship between the two societies. The special relationship of the UK and Germany defines additional duties which do not apply to citizens of Afghanistan.

I.4.e.iii Societies have obligations to other societies.

The pattern of exchange and interaction does not stop within a single society, and societies have many points of contact with other societies, as well as with persons beyond their frontiers. In the same way as groups can have relationships with other groups (▶ I.2.a.iii), societies can have relationships with other societies. If social groups from one society interact with social groups from another, each of those groups is likely to develop obligations to others. The most obvious example is that of business and commerce; between two trading nations, contractual relationships are formed in their thousands. This is not directly equivalent to the obligation of the whole society, though whenever there is a sufficiently large number of such relationships, it can be difficult in practice to distinguish between the actions of groups within society and the actions of the society itself. Foreign direct investment plays a major part in the economies of developing countries; it is important for those countries because it brings in resources, expertise and revenue, while helping to incorporate the society into the economic market. At the same time, it can stifle local competition, milk a poor economy of its product and focus production on items which do not serve local needs.[125] It is possible to

---

125 M. Todaro (1994) *Economic development*, New York: Longman, ch. 15.

argue that these are not issues for the societies which they affect, but the position is difficult to sustain.

This kind of problem becomes an issue for the whole society when it is identified as a social matter. This statement has a certain circularity about it, but it reflects the general argument that what people believe to be true in a society is true in its consequences. If people identify themselves with armies, with businesses, with sports teams, or – however implausibly – with individual citizens, the issues become social issues.

I.4.e.iv   Societies have obligations to previous generations.

If people have obligations to past and future generations (▶ I.1.c.ii(3)), the same is true of societies. Society, Edmund Burke wrote, is a partnership: 'a partnership not only between those who are living, but between those who are living, those who are dead, and those who are to be born'.[126] The statement, long associated with a conservative view of society, seems almost mystical; it defines a society as a partnership of ghosts. The main responsibility which is recognized to past generations is a simple one: to accept the decisions which are made until they are changed through a formal process. Laws and treaties are respected until they are changed, no matter how fatuous they may have become; property rights are treated as continuous (they do not have to be: the biblical 'jubilee' traditionally wiped out rights over land every fifty years). Some commentators have argued for compensation for wrongs perpetrated by previous generations (the basis of arguments for compensation for native Americans, Maoris and indigenous Australians, or the association of modern day racism with slavery). The argument is a direct corollary of the view that we should accept the distribution which results from our ancestors' actions, which is why it is accepted by neo-liberals.[127]

Beyond this, though, we also accept obligations imposed by previous generations on the basis of reciprocity: war pensions are an obvious example. Less obviously, the provision of health care for elderly people, the development of educational provision and the maintenance of the infrastructure of public services are legacies of the past, framed as obligations because the benefits have already been received.

I.4.e.v   Societies have obligations to future generations.

The basic responsibility a society has to future generations extends beyond its responsibility to the past. The main responsibility to the past is the responsibility of a custodian; the task is to preserve, protect and

---

126 E. Burke (1790) *Reflections on the revolution in France*, New York: Holt, Rinehart and Winston, 1959, p. 117.
127 R. Nozick (1974) *Anarchy, state and utopia*, Oxford: Blackwell.

pass on what has been received. Responsibilities to the future are conditioned by the actions of people in the past; the principle of generalized reciprocity implies that the efforts which have been made for this generation carry an obligation to do as much for the next.

The classic expression of these responsibilities is the duty of stewardship – a commitment not just to preserve, but to improve and build on the things we have. Stewards work in co-operation with nature, to improve and perfect it; a typical image of the steward is of someone who plants a tree for the use of future generations. This is not, however, a 'green' principle, in the sense in which that is commonly understood. Stewards do not just maintain or conserve; they change, they build, they improve, and they have a duty to do so. Stewardship is an ancient idea; Passmore attributes it to the post-Platonic philosophers of the Roman empire,[128] and it can be found in traditional Christianity (in, for example, the parable of the talents) and in Islam. The obligations of stewardship are held both to the past, to conserve and cherish the best, and to the future, to develop and to build.

The responsibility to future generations has broad implications. Solidarity can be used to define the limits of obligations, as well as the obligations themselves; one reason why people in developing countries continue to experience avoidable deprivation is precisely that they are not included in the pattern of obligation and entitlement which I have described. The recognition of responsibility to future generations brings with it elements of uncertainty. From what we know about a society, we may have some idea of future development – what is the heritage we are leaving them, whether the members of a society will be relatively advantaged or disadvantaged in their relations with other countries, or what language they will speak. But we cannot know what their life-style will be, what they will see as being in their interests, or even what their culture may be.

This seems to me to come very close to the problem that John Rawls poses: how to distribute goods fairly when we do not know what the consequences will be.[129] Although I do not share many of Rawls's value judgements, I recognize that the strategy he proposes – 'maximin', or maximizing the minimum – could be an effective way of protecting the prospects of unborn generations. This is qualified mainly because the knowledge that people have of their own circumstances, and the current state of the world, might incline them to take risks, or make judgements about future developments. The safest strategy is one which promotes the best minimum conditions overall.

This is not quite the same as a general obligation of solidarity, but it does imply that solidaristic obligations have a much wider scope than

---

128 J. Passmore (1974) *Man's responsibility for nature*, London: Duckworth, ch. 2.
129 J. Rawls (1971) *A theory of justice*, Oxford: Oxford University Press.

might at first appear. We can only protect future generations effectively – and so, fulfil our obligations to them – by seeking to protect everyone in the circumstances in which they are likely to be found. The condition of the environment, the development of the global economy and the social relationships we promote are basic to the circumstances of the people we do accept responsibility for as well as those we don't. A commitment to the future cannot be confined to a specific and identifiable group of people.

I.4.e.vi   Societies can be moral agents.

Saying that societies have moral obligations is not directly equivalent to saying that a society is a moral agent, because to be a moral agent there has to be a formal structure which can accept and act on moral responsibilities. A family can have moral obligations, but the family does not have the formal structure which would make moral agency possible. A business, by contrast, usually does have such a structure. This is why it is possible to treat a business as a corporate person, and to treat directors as personally responsible for the conduct of the business. Societies often have such a formal structure, through the political system, and in consequence it is through the political system that moral agency is liable to be expressed. The relationship of a society to its political system has still to be discussed, and the point will be returned to in due course.

II WELFARE

II Welfare is obtained and maintained through social action.

THE NATURE OF WELFARE

II.1 People have needs, which require a social response.

Welfare
II.1.a	*Well-being requires certain needs to be met.*
II.1.a.i	Needs are socially constructed.
II.1.a.ii	Needs go beyond the essentials for survival.
II.1.a.iii	Well-being requires more than the satisfaction of needs.
II.1.a.iv	Social groups also experience well-being, or the lack of it.

Poverty and exclusion
II.1.b	*Welfare is vitiated by poverty and exclusion.*
II.1.b.i	Poverty is the converse of welfare.
II.1.b.ii	Exclusion denies well-being.
II.1.b.iii	Poverty and exclusion are moral issues.

Responding to need
II.1.c	*Needs present obligations to other people.*
II.1.c.i	Society defines the acceptable minimum.
II.1.c.ii	The obligation to people who are poor and excluded is often weak.
II.1.c.iii	The response to poverty and exclusion must be social.

Welfare

II.1.a Well-being requires certain needs to be met.

Welfare is an ambiguous term. It is used to refer both to people's well-being, and to systems which are designed to provide for people. For the moment, I shall confine myself to the former use of the term. At the level of the person, well-being depends on a wide range of factors, both negative and positive. The negative factors are things which should not be done to people – such as murder, arbitrary confinement, pollution of the person's environment, and so forth. The positive factors are things which should be present for people to experience well-being. At the most basic level they include the physical necessities of life, like water, food and air, and the goods and materials necessary to ordinary life, like clothing and fuel. But they also include many social factors, including interaction with other people, affection, security and personal development.

The negative factors are commonly discussed in the language of rights, and they will be returned to in those terms later. The positive factors are needs, in the sense that they are necessary for people; people cannot live well if their needs are not met. The effect of a failure to meet any one of these needs – for example for water, shelter, security or affiliation – is that this factor, or the lack of it, comes to dominate the person's life. Needs are necessary to well-being; without them, well-being is vitiated. Feinberg argues that these factors are essential to the person;[130] someone who does not have them will find it difficult if not impossible to function as a person.

II.1.a.i Needs are socially constructed.

Needs are things which are 'necessary' for a person. Needs commonly refer to things that people do not have. They are often represented in terms of deprivation, or as problems, but they mean more than this: needs refer to things that people must have, or to conditions which have to be met. A need has to be a need for something.

There has been a long debate about what is and what is not necessary for people. It has often been bitter, because of the fear of each party that the kinds of need they are most concerned about may be forgotten or ignored if another definition is accepted.[131] Advocates of an 'absolute' view have argued that needs apply irrespective of social circumstances or conditions,[132] while advocates of a 'relative' view have argued that the

---

130 E.g. J. Feinberg (1973) *Social philosophy*, Englewood Cliffs, NJ: Prentice-Hall.

131 A. Sen (1983) 'Poor, relatively speaking', *Oxford Economic Papers*, 35: 153–169; P. Townsend (1985) 'A sociological approach to the measurement of poverty – a rejoinder to Professor Amartya Sen', *Oxford Economic Papers*, 37: 659–668; A. Sen (1985) 'A sociological approach to the measurement of poverty: a reply to Professor Peter Townsend', *Oxford Economic Papers*, 37: 669–676.

132 E.g. V. George (1988) *Wealth, poverty and starvation*, Hemel Hempstead: Wheatsheaf Books, p. 208.

standards depend on the society in which they occur.[133] Both are correct, in different ways. We need certain things in order to live, like food, water, shelter or warmth. But the way in which these things are provided and obtained depends on the society we live in. What constitutes 'food' depends on what it is acceptable to eat: people in different societies feel differently about eating horses, insects, snakes or pigs, and these things may or may not be classifiable as 'food'. The definition of shelter depends on the society; in the UK, temporary shelters and shanties are generally illegal and liable to closure. Warmth can be achieved in several ways – through activity, through clothing, and through the use of fuel. Activity consumes calories, and so requires food; clothing requires material; and there are many types of fuel, including coal, oil, gas, wood and so forth. In Sen's terms, there may be a core of absolute need, but the commodities which are needed, and the characteristics of those commodities, are socially determined.[134]

II.1.a.ii Needs go beyond the essentials for survival.

The idea of need has been used to refer to the essentials for basic survival, but the boundaries of need are hazy, and every attempt to define need in a restricted way has gradually been expanded to include further kinds of need. It is not enough to talk about the minimum necessary for survival, because people are able to survive in widely different circumstances, even where they are starved, beaten and dehumanized. The idea of 'subsistence' was introduced to refer to 'mere physical efficiency'[135] – a level of living at which people would not be malnourished, cold or sick. But this standard is too restrictive to be useful in practice. People are social beings, and a standard which does not allow them to protect themselves against harm, to interact with other people or to form relationships fails to relate to many of the most essential needs. The United Nations has sought to develop a concept of 'basic needs', which extends the idea of subsistence to include certain social needs, including for example education and health cover.[136] As this process goes on, it becomes clear that what people need extends far beyond the basic minimum necessary for survival or subsistence. People need cars, schools or electricity, not because these things are intrinsic to humanity, but because they live in societies where these things are essential.

---

133 P. Townsend (1993) *The international analysis of poverty*, Hemel Hempstead: Harvester Wheatsheaf.

134 Sen (1983), p. 160.

135 B.S. Rowntree (1922) *Poverty: a study of town life*, new edition, London: Longmans.

136 United Nations Development Program (1990) *Human Development Report 1990: concepts and measurement of human development*, New York: Oxford University Press.

II.1.a.iii Well-being requires more than the satisfaction of needs.

Needs are not sufficient for well-being: more factors contribute to welfare than the satisfaction of basic material needs. Maslow wrote of a 'hierarchy' of needs: physiological needs were most basic, followed by needs for safety, love, esteem and self-actualization.[137] The order of priority Maslow gives the factors is very disputable, and it is not certain that a hierarchy can be strictly defined: the needs he describes are interlinked. What does seem to be true is that people have needs at different levels, and that as some needs are met, others are liable to become apparent.

People whose basic needs are met are not necessarily content, and they may come to see other desires – a larger house, a better car, a more active social life – as important to their lives. The issue is not just that people are insatiable; achieving personal goals and ambitions also matters. In other words, people want to have their needs met, and then they want some more. Economic theory tends to focus on what people want – or more precisely, what they choose to have – rather than what they need. Assessments of need are commonly made in terms of what we think is good for people, or what they ought to have; people's 'utility' – their happiness, or what they think is good for them – is measured in terms of what people choose to have. Clearly, there is a considerable cross-over between these concepts, because many people will choose to have what they need. The economic analysis usually works well enough in practice, partly because it deals with the preferences of the 'average' person rather than any real person, and partly because it is most commonly applied in developed societies, in which basic needs are likely to be met. That means that the needs which have still to be met tend to be at higher levels – including psychological needs, and the satisfaction of aspirations. The ability to choose is fundamental to these needs.

II.1.a.iv Social groups also experience well-being, or the lack of it.

Well-being is not only experienced by persons; it can also be said to be experienced by social groups. A group is not the same as a number of people, and the welfare of a group cannot simply be determined by aggregating the welfare of the individuals who make it up.

It is possible to show formally that rational individual preferences do not necessarily yield a rational group preference. The formal proof developed by the Marquis de Condorcet is simple enough. A rational preference is transitive (if x is preferred to y, and y to z, then x is

---

137 A.H. Maslow (1943) 'A theory of human motivation', *Psychological Review*, 50: 395.

Table 1   *The Condorcet problem*

	Person A	Person B	Person C
Health	1	2	3
Education	2	3	1
Housing	3	1	2

preferred to z) and non-reflexive (if x is preferred to y, y is not preferred to x). Imagine that three people are given three choices for priorities in spending, and put them in the order of priority outlined in Table 1. A majority (A and B) prefer health to education. A majority (A and C) prefer education to housing. But a majority (C and B) prefer housing to health, which is inconsistent with the other choices. This means that consistent individual preferences have yielded an inconsistent majority decision.

Arrow's 'impossibility theorem' claims to show on this basis that it is impossible to identify the welfare of a group on the basis of individual preferences without dictatorship – imposing preferences on those who think differently.[138] But Arrow's proof depends on the assumption of 'unrestricted domain', the supposition that any combination of preferences might be adopted. In real life, this is unlikely. Because people are socialized into similar sets of views and values, it is not impossible that everyone might be of the same mind. There is little serious disagreement that children should be raised in families, that people should be able to buy food, or that health is better than sickness, and it has not taken the action of a dictator to produce the agreement. If everyone is of the same mind, the interests of the group and the interests of the person within the group cannot be distinguished. At the same time, it has to be accepted that groups do not in general consist of people with identical positions, interests and preferences; on the contrary, most social groups rely on some differentiation of roles and position within the group. There will be differences, and where they occur there are often conflicts or disagreements.

Irrespective of the position of individuals within a group, the group has interests as a group. These interests may be quite distinct from the interests of the people within it, except in so far as they are members of the group. It is generally in the interests of a social group – like a family, a community or a nation – to continue to exist. It is generally considered to be in the interests of a nation to defend itself against attack, even where some people within it suffer directly as a result.

The fostering of group interests is generally described in terms of 'cohesion' (▶ I.2.b.i). The links which are formed between members of the

---

138 K. Arrow (1967) 'Values and collective decision-making', in E.S. Phelps (ed.) *Economic justice*, Harmondsworth: Penguin, 1973.

group are generally links of solidarity, and the connection between solidarity and social cohesion is a direct one; a cohesive group or society is one in which people feel responsibility to each other (▶ I.3.c).

Poverty and exclusion

II.1.b   Welfare is vitiated by poverty and exclusion.

The term 'poverty' is generally used to describe circumstances in which people suffer serious deficiencies in their material needs. Someone who is poor lacks well-being. Exclusion consists primarily of a lack of integration into solidaristic social networks (▶ I.3.c.iii), which might occur because of social rejection or because of a lack of social ties. The excluded person is unable to meet needs which depend on relationships with other people in society – a large part of a person's needs overall.

Poverty and exclusion are paradigmatic cases of need. They are not the only cases: people can have other serious needs which disrupt their well-being – a house which is flooded, a life-threatening illness, being subject to crime. They may not even be the most important; terrible as poverty and exclusion can be, there are still worse things that can happen. They are paradigmatic mainly because they are commonplace: poverty and exclusion account for many of the serious, extreme or persistent needs which have become the focus of social policy. As such, they are fundamental to much of the discussion of welfare.

II.1.b.i   *Poverty is the converse of welfare.*

Poverty is a much-used, and ambiguous, concept. It refers to a wide range of problems, including problems in material conditions, economic circumstances and social relationships.[139] Material conditions include deprivation of basic needs; a low standard of living; and multiple deprivation. Material need is understood as a lack of material goods, such as food, clothing, fuel or shelter, which people require in order to live and function in society. A low standard of living refers to the general experience of living with fewer resources and lower consumption than other people. Multiple deprivation refers to circumstances in which people suffer from a constellation of deprivations associated with limited resources experienced over a period of time. Poverty is not defined, on this account, by any specific need (like hunger or homelessness), but by the existence of a pattern of deprivation.

The economic circumstances include a lack of resources; inequality; and low class. A lack of resources refers to circumstances in which

---

139 P. Spicker (1999) 'Definitions of poverty: eleven clusters of meaning', in D. Gordon and P. Spicker (eds) *International glossary of poverty*, London: Zed Books.

people do not have the income, wealth or resources to acquire the things they need. Poverty is understood in terms of inequality when people are disadvantaged by comparison with others in society; people whose economic situation is very much inferior to others are liable to be unable to participate in society.[140] A 'class' of people is a group identified by virtue of their economic position in society. In Marxian analyses, classes are defined by their relationship to the means of production, and in developed countries poor people are primarily those who are marginalized within the economic system. In the Weberian sense, classes refer to people in distinct economic categories: poverty constitutes a class either when it establishes distinct categories of social relationship (like exclusion or dependency), or when the situation of poor people is identifiably distinguishable from others.

The social relationships cover exclusion, dependency and lack of security. A concept of poverty identified with exclusion sees it as the inability to participate in the normal pattern of social life. The European Union defines poverty as exclusion resulting from limited resources:

> The poor shall be taken as to mean persons, families and groups of persons whose resources (material, cultural and social) are so limited as to exclude them from the minimum acceptable way of life in the Member State in which they live.[141]

The relationship of poor people to dependency assumes that poor people receive social benefits in consequence of their lack of means. The sociologist Georg Simmel argued that 'poverty', in sociological terms, referred not to all people on low incomes but to those who were dependent.[142] Poverty is equivalent to lack of security when it implies vulnerability to social risks. Charles Booth referred to poor people as 'living under a struggle to obtain the necessaries of life and make both ends meet; while the "very poor" live in a state of chronic want'.[143]

These different uses of the term have no constant element in common, though they are linked by a strong family resemblance; a person can suffer from material conditions, economic deprivation and impaired social relationships together, and in fact these phenomena are intimately connected.

---

140 M. O'Higgins and S. Jenkins (1990) 'Poverty in the EC: 1975, 1980, 1985', in R. Teekens and B. van Praag (eds) *Analysing poverty in the European Community* (*Eurostat News* Special Edition 1-1990), Luxembourg: European Communities.

141 Council Decision of 19 February 1984, cited D. Ramprakesh (1994) 'Poverty in the countries of the European Union', *Journal of European Social Policy*, 4 (2): 117–128.

142 G. Simmel (1908) 'The poor', *Social Problems*, 13 (1965): 118–139.

143 C. Booth (1902) *Life and Labour of the People in London*, Macmillan, First Series: Poverty, vol 1, p. 33.

The relationship of poverty to welfare is not straightforward, because the concept of poverty itself is not straightforward. If poverty is taken to mean a low income, it may be possible to have a low income while maintaining an adequate standard of living; if it refers to dependency, it is possible to be dependent and to have one's needs met. But most senses of the term 'poverty' imply a degree of hardship or suffering, and that is the converse of well-being.

II.1.b.ii   Exclusion denies well-being.

Exclusion can arise for many reasons, not all of them associated with poverty; people can be excluded because of physical differences, racial status or moral disapproval. Exclusion has the effect of exposing people to hardship.[144] If there are barriers to interacting with other people, there are fewer opportunities to develop and to pursue one's objectives. People who suffer exclusion over any period of time have a limited ability to participate in society, and in this sense exclusion may be directly analogous to poverty.

The problems of exclusion go beyond poverty, though, in their implications for the person. Social identity is conditioned and formed through the type and character of the social contact which people experience (▸ I.1.b). It determines the structure of obligations which relate to a person, and so the degree of support which that person may expect to receive when the need arises. And it can be seen, in itself, as an indication of the quality of social life, because it is largely from our social relationships and roles that we achieve the goals and engage in the kind of activities we think are worthwhile. Exclusion directly denies social well-being, because it implies that the person is cut off from the sources of well-being (▸ I.3.c.iii).

II.1.b.iii   Poverty and exclusion are moral issues.

The idea of poverty has a strong evaluative and moral element. People are considered poor when their situation or standard of living falls below the level which is considered acceptable. Attempts to define poverty in objective and scientific terms have failed, David Piachaud argues, because the moral ground shifts.[145] Poverty consists of unacceptable hardship; the key term here is 'unacceptable', because what that means depends on the codes and values prevalent in a particular society at a particular time.

---

144 S. Tiemann (1993) Opinion on social exclusion, Brussels: Commission of the European Communities, OJ 93/C 352/13.

145 D. Piachaud (1981) 'Peter Townsend and the Holy Grail', New Society, 10 September: 421.

Exclusion is a moral issue in a slightly different sense. A person who is excluded is not part of solidaristic social networks; such a person is outside many of the normal structures of moral obligation which bind people together in society. This can happen because of poverty, deviance, social rejection, or the absence of social ties; but, whatever the reason, the excluded person in a sense falls outside a society. That is a moral problem in itself; on occasions, too (notably in the French discourse on 'marginality'),[146] it is coupled with concern that the person who is not part of a society may not have reason to respect its norms. Either position furthers a moral argument for action against exclusion, or 'social inclusion'.

Responding to need

II.1.c Needs present obligations to other people.

Needs are claims. A claim of need is a normative statement about the way in which people should be treated.[147] People who can meet needs from their own resources do not have to make a claim; but wherever needs are not met, a claim is established against others.

Who are the 'others' against whom the claim is being made? There is no single, straightforward answer, and it depends on the context – needs for health care are often seen as different from claims for housing. Some people have entitlements which are sufficient to guarantee the satisfaction of a need; some do not.[148] When a small child needs to be fed, the immediate assumption is likely to be made that it is the responsibility of its parents. When a person becomes too ill to work, the responsibilities may fall on family, employers or workmates, depending on the structure of obligations. Even if a person is run over in the street, there are general responsibilities applying to people in the vicinity, strangers or not (▶ I.3.a.ii). The structure of these obligations reflects the general structure of obligations in a society, and the patterns of exchange, reciprocity and moral obligation which apply elsewhere (▶ I.1.c.i, I.3.a). Ultimately, when no other obligation has hierarchical precedence, the claim of need has to rely on the broadest sense of generalized reciprocity, and that makes it a claim against a society.

---

146 See e.g. E. Mossé (1986) *Les Riches et les pauvres*, Paris: Editions du Seuil; P. Nasse, H. Strohl and M. Xiberras (1992) *Exclus et exclusions*, Paris: Commissariat du Plan; S. Paugam (1993) *La Disqualification sociale: essai sur la nouvelle pauvreté*, Paris: Presses Universitaires de France.

147 P. Spicker (1993) 'Needs as claims', *Social Policy and Administration*, 27 (1): 7–17.

148 J. Drèze and A. Sen (1989) *Hunger and public action*, Oxford: Clarendon Press.

The establishment of a 'need' is not, however, decisive; demanding a response is not the same thing as getting it. Needs are only one type of claim: other claims might be based on personal obligation, merit, morality or rights. Equally, claims based on need can be denied for a range of reasons, including moral principles, a limited ability to pay, or conflicting duties (including competing claims of need).

II.1.c.i   Society defines the acceptable minimum.

The norms which are prevalent in a society depend on the society of which they are part. The expectations which people have, and their perception of normality, depend on the patterns of social contact, the development of intersubjective ideas, and the process of socialization (▶ I.1.c). Taken naively, that might seem to suggest that there is a process almost like voting, in which people are consulted as to what they think essential, and a consensus emerges about the level of need. Of course the process is nothing like this, but it is interesting to note that some very successful research has been based on just this method.[149] Asking people what they think in opinion polls or focus groups is a way of tapping into a rich vein of intersubjective views – views which are not formed in isolation, but through a process of interaction and socialization.

In the same way, a society defines an acceptable minimum. There are two discrete stages in the process – discrete, but not distinct. First, the need itself, which Sen calls the 'lack of capability',[150] is socially defined. The importance of issues like transport, shelter or communications depends crucially on the kind of society one lives in. Second, the ways in which the needs might be met – the commodities – are identified socially. Ultimately, a strictly 'absolute' view is not sustainable, partly because the responses which needs call for are socially determined, but also because the needs themselves are conditioned and constructed socially.

The development of social norms is not the same as the development of social obligations; it does not follow, because society determines the standard, that society must accept responsibility for it. But it does at least add weight to claims based on need if they are socially accepted and sanctioned.

II.1.c.ii   The obligation to people who are poor and excluded is often weak.

The people who are most in need are often people to whom existing obligations are weakest. Obligations diminish with social distance

---

149 J. Mack and S. Lansley (1985) *Poor Britain*, London: George Allen and Unwin; J. Veit-Wilson (1987) 'Consensual approaches to poverty lines and social security', *Journal of Social Policy*, 16 (2): 183–211.
150 Sen (1983).

(► I.3.a.i). Exclusion implies, virtually by definition, that such obligations do not exist. Poverty implies an inability to participate in society, which means that fewer social ties and mutual obligations apply to poor people than to others. It follows, then, that those who have the most serious needs are less likely than others to have those needs met. The process is visible in many countries, where there is protection of a relatively privileged inner group (the 'garantismo' of Southern Europe) and exclusion of a significant number of people at the margins.

This points to a central weakness in the structure I have outlined, and a key moral problem in the development of social policy. For those who are concerned about welfare in its own right, poverty and exclusion are fundamentally important; but they are also the circumstances in which the existing structure of obligations seems to be least active.

II.1.c.iii The response to poverty and exclusion must be social.

It is possible that nothing at all might be done about poverty or exclusion. It is in the nature of the problems that people do not necessarily have obligations towards poor or excluded people, and they can remain in need, or be left to their own devices.

Three considerations work against this. The first is the social dimension. Exclusion and poverty have implications for social cohesion which go beyond the interests of the people who are poor or excluded (► I.3.c). The second consideration is the moral dimension of poverty and exclusion (► II.1.b.iii). Third, there are social principles, in particular the principle of generalized reciprocity, which imply some responsibility towards poor or excluded people (► I.1.c.i). A striking finding from the anthropological literature is that societies do not, in general, leave poor people without support: the principle of giving to the poor is widespread.[151]

Although none of these principles is conclusive in itself, it seems clear that there may be a response to poverty and exclusion, and there is a moral case to argue that there should be. Where such a response is made, it has to be social – because, where there are no particular obligations (that is, obligations relating to particular individuals), only general social obligations exist.

---

151 M. Sahlins (1974) *Stone age economics*, London: Tavistock.

THE PRECONDITIONS FOR WELFARE

II.2 People have economic and social rights.

Economic development
II.2.a	*Welfare depends on economic development.*
II.2.a.i	Economic development requires an appropriately structured economy.
II.2.a.ii	Welfare also requires the avoidance of poverty.

Basic security
II.2.b	*Security is concerned with welfare in the future, as well as the present.*
II.2.b.i	Change implies insecurity.
II.2.b.ii	Those who are most vulnerable to insecurity are those who are poorest.
II.2.b.iii	Social insecurity requires social protection.

The structure of rights
II.2.c	*Rights are essential to welfare.*
II.2.c.i	Freedom is a precondition for well-being.
II.2.c.ii	Political protection is required to guarantee welfare.
II.2.c.iii	Economic and social rights are preconditions for well-being.
II.2.c.iv	Rights exist.

Economic development

II.2.a Welfare depends on economic development.

Well-being cannot simply be reduced to material issues (▸ II.1.a), and it would be false to assume that an increase in material goods auto-matically yields an improvement in welfare. It is easy to gain a different impression from economic theory, because most marginal analysis assumes preferences for increasing material consumption. But these preferences are developed on a previously identified structure of individual choices; choices which are morally unacceptable, or inconsistent with the pattern of social life, have been effectively excluded before the marginal analysis begins.

Economic development is not sufficient for welfare, but it is necessary, because it is basic to material welfare. In part, this is because it is only through economic development that some of the most serious issues in welfare can ever be addressed. A large minority of the world's population still lacks water supplies, sewerage and facilities for the drainage of surface water;[152] the provision of these very basic facilities is a form of economic development. In part, too, it is because the expansion of production is necessary to give people the power to exchange, and so to avail themselves of the goods and services which might enhance their lives.

Economic development is requisite for welfare, however, in three ways. First, material goods are essential for people to live and to prosper. There is a prominent argument for 'sustainable' growth,[153] which often is taken to mean minimal growth. The condition of people in severely undeveloped regions is not sustainable, and the prime effect of attempts to restrict growth is to put a fetter on the poor.

Second, economic development is essential to social integration. Involvement in economic activity and exchange is a major determinant of the development of social relationships beyond an immediate circle. This applies not only to a person who is directly involved, but to others in the same household.

Third, being able to improve their circumstances is fundamental to the achievement of people's aims. Without economic growth, improvement can be achieved only through the reduction of inefficiency (for which opportunities may be limited) or at the expense of other people.

At the same time, economic development generates its own casualties: for example, people whose relative earning capacity is extinguished, who become vulnerable to market fluctuations, and those who are displaced because of development. Development is not an unalloyed good for everyone concerned, and mechanisms have to be introduced to protect people from its negative consequences.

---

152 J. Hardoy, S. Cairncross and D. Satterthwaite (eds) (1990) *The poor die young*, London: Earthscan.

153 Club of Rome (1972) *The limits to growth*, New York: Universe Books; D.H. Meadows, D.L. Meadows and J. Randers (1992) *Beyond the limits*, London: Earthscan.

II.2.a.i   Economic development requires an appropriately structured economy.

Economic development can happen spontaneously, through growth over time. Historically, this is what happened in most of the developed countries, though it largely did so from a base of relative economic security and power. It is tempting, then, to assume that economic development can be spontaneously generated in all cases. The problem with this is that there are routes to industrialization which preclude adequate development or further progress.[154]

The 'structure' of an economy is, like the structure of society, a construct. The reference to 'structure' does not mean that the economy is designed; it means that the elements of the economy have a systematic relationship to each other. Mechanisms for exchange, finance and communications are needed for development to be possible. This is the core of the World Bank's attempts to foster 'structural adjustment' programmes, developing economies through the encouragement of rules allowing for financial stability, flexibility in markets and responsiveness to industrial demands. But this approach has often led to hardship for the less developed countries, and in particular for the poorest people in them.[155] Cypher and Dietz argue on this basis that structural transformation is probably better achieved through distortion, and perhaps even replacement, of market processes.[156]

II.2.a.ii   Welfare also requires the avoidance of poverty.

Development is insufficient to protect people from material hardship. Within the framework of development, there has to be consideration of the welfare of those who are poor. It is possible to represent economic development as the avoidance of poverty, and so as a means of obtaining welfare, but there is a degree of circularity in that argument: if poverty is a lack of welfare, developing resources is equivalent to improving welfare. This is too narrow a view of welfare, and too narrow a view of poverty.

Poverty and welfare are complex concepts, relating not only to material conditions but more generally to economic and social circumstances (► II.1.b.i). The prevention of poverty can be taken to include improvement in people's material conditions; economic development is directed towards that end. It may also, however, depend on altering social relationships, and it may imply changes in the moral status of the poor. These elements go beyond the issue of economic development.

---

154 J. Cypher and J. Dietz (1997) *The process of economic development*, London: Routledge.

155 F. Stewart (1995) *Adjustment and poverty*, London: Routledge.

156 Cypher and Dietz (1997), p. 284.

Basic security

II.2.b Security is concerned with welfare in the future, as well as the present.

Security is part of welfare. It is important not only that people should be able to obtain and use goods and services, but that the process should be, at least to a reasonable extent, predictable. Security is a basic need, in the sense that it is essential to a person; like other needs, the effect of its denial comes to dominate and overwhelm other parts of a person's life. Poverty has been identified with a lack of basic security (▶ II.1.b.i):

> chronic poverty results when the lack of basic security simultaneously affects several aspects of people's lives, when it is prolonged, and when it seriously compromises people's chances of regaining their rights and of resuming their responsibilities in the foreseeable future.[157]

The United Nations Development Program has argued for a wide interpretation of the idea of security, to cover a range of factors: economic security, food, health, environmental security, personal security, community security and political security.[158] This is a strategic argument – an attempt to broaden the focus of governments already committed to protecting the security of their citizens. In this section, though, I want to take a more limited view of the idea of security. This is not to deny the validity of the broader concept, but most of the issues have been dealt with in different ways.

The essence of a discussion of security, rather than basic needs, is that it concerns the future – the question of what may happen. People are at risk when negative things may happen. They are vulnerable when they are likely to suffer as a result. (These points are separable: risk relates to the range of contingencies, vulnerability to the seriousness of their consequences.) These issues relate not just to material conditions, but to expectations. One person reasonably may feel insecure in a relatively stable, unchanging environment; another may feel secure in shifting circumstances. This is not just a question of subjective appraisal; in labour markets which require flexibility, a person with a stable work record may be more vulnerable than another person with wider employment experience and greater adaptability.

---

157 Wresinski Report of the Economic and Social Council of France (1987) cited in K. Duffy (1995) *Social exclusion and human dignity in Europe*, Council of Europe CDPS(95) 1 Rev, p. 36.

158 United Nations Development Program (1994) *Human development report 1994*, Oxford: Oxford University Press, pp. 24–33.

II.2.b.i Change implies insecurity.

When things change, people may become vulnerable. The improvements in material status which accompany economic development have also often been accompanied by insecurity. The effect of moving to the market is to require specialization in production; specialization may make people richer, but it also makes them more vulnerable to change, because they have less protection against adverse circumstances.[159] There is an irony here: this sort of change is often basic to improvements in material circumstances. It has also been essential in the movement from traditional, status-based societies to economically developed societies. Security is not an unequivocal good; change is essential if people's aspirations are to be met. The main issues concern the pace of change, and the degree of protection available to people when it happens.

II.2.b.ii Those who are most vulnerable to insecurity are those who are poorest.

Security has to be understood in the context of the society where it occurs. Expectations are developed in terms of social status (▶ I.2.c.i). A person's social position depends on the social structure; it relates to the set of social roles which a person plays, and roles in turn consist of expectations about what a person does in society. Because expectations are conditioned by status, and a sense of security is conditioned by such expectations, status conditions a sense of security. Many expectations about the future, and perceptions of risk, are founded in perceptions of social roles and status; status fosters expectations about occupation, career, life-style, income, leisure and social relationships. Evidently enough, someone with no educational or career prospects is likely to regard the future differently from someone who is socially and materially privileged.

Social status is not a simple guarantee of security; some high-status occupations also involve high risks, and exposure to considerable changes of fortune, even as some low-status occupations are relatively well established and secure. What is true, however, is that people in different economic and social positions are affected differently by this insecurity. Economic position makes it possible to protect against insecurity, through savings, investment or insurance. Social position can be a means of making contacts and placing oneself to avoid future hardship.

This leads to the situation where poorer people are liable to be more vulnerable than others, even if the risks they face seem similar. In practice, however, their position is also liable to be less secure. The

---

159 P. Streeten (1995) 'Comments on "The framework of ILO action against poverty"', in G. Rodgers (ed.) *The poverty agenda and the ILO*, Geneva: International Labour Office.

development of labour-saving technology has meant that unskilled and semi-skilled labour is available in abundance, and lower paid workers have been relegated to a peripheral status. There is, for poorer workers, a risk of 'sub-employment', in which they move continually between marginal and temporary labour and unemployment.[160] In France, this situation is referred to as *précarité*, or precariousness.

The effect of poverty is a diminution in the range of options which are available to a person. 'It is not the poverty of my people which appals me,' Aneurin Bevan once commented, 'it is the poverty of their choice.' People who have fewer and harder choices are more vulnerable than others, because the effect of losing any further options is to limit their potential outcomes to a greater extent.

II.2.b.iii   Social insecurity requires social protection.

Social insecurity represents a challenge to welfare. Even if people's basic needs are met, the prospect of changing to a situation where they might not be met is liable to be a major concern. The principal sources of insecurity in developed countries are probably concerns with old age, sickness and disability, though others are also important, like fear of crime, unemployment or business failure, and divorce.

People can attempt to limit their insecurity by insuring against a range of contingencies. The ability to do so within the constraints of each person's resources is, however, limited. This has led to the development of systems of mutual aid and, in particular the pooling of risk. These systems are the basis of 'social protection'. It is protection, rather than a form of service, because it is contingent: people benefit from it only if they experience the circumstances for which it is designed. It is social because it depends on other people in order to work.

The structure of rights

II.2.c   Rights are essential to welfare.

A right is a norm, held to inhere in the person who possesses it and affecting the behaviour of others towards that person. In principle, this is often equivalent to an obligation, because the effect of someone holding an obligation to another person can be directly equivalent to the situation where the other person has a right. Rights do not necessarily imply duties; my right to walk down the street unmolested does not place any

---

160 D. Matza and H. Miller (1976) 'Poverty and proletariat', in R.K. Merton and R. Nisbet (eds) *Contemporary social problems*, 4th edition, New York: Harcourt Brace Jovanovich, pp. 639–675.

obligation on another person, but comes into play only when the right is breached. Many important civil rights – like freedom of speech or freedom of assembly – are rights of this kind; they are 'liberties'.[161]

The role which rights play in relation to welfare is partly negative: the possession of a right means that people will not act in certain ways towards the bearer of the right. It may also be positive: having a right can mean that people will act in ways which benefit that person directly. When people talk about 'the rights of children', for example, the rights in question may be both negative and positive. In negative terms, the rights of children include rights not to be abused or neglected, and not to be exploited. In positive terms, they include the right of children to be educated. These positive rights are also referred to as 'claim rights', because they imply that a claim can be made, morally or legally, against someone who has the obligation to provide them.

Both negative and positive rights – liberties and claim rights – are necessary to well-being. They are not necessary in the theoretical sense of the term. It is conceivable that someone could develop into a person without them, and that such a person might still have a degree of well-being. However, their absence would call into question the kind of well-being the person could have, and they are certainly necessary in practice. The central problem is that where there are no rights, there are no means to protect well-being, and no reason why well-being should not be denied to someone. The absence of liberties does not mean that there will be no freedom of action, but it does mean that there might be none. Similarly, the absence of claim rights or obligations does not mean that children will fail to be educated or to be protected by their families, but only that they might be. In practice, inevitably, this will apply to some people, and it is for those people that these rights are essential.

This is where individualism comes into play. People who are left out are precisely those who need rights the most. In principle, it may be possible to guarantee rights by appointing someone to protect those who are vulnerable. This happens, for example, when parents are given the right to act on a child's behalf. But it often happens that the person against whom vulnerable people have to be protected is the same person who has been invested with their rights: children need protection from abusive parents,[162] residents in institutions need protection against their carers,[163] and so on. One of the most effective ways of guaranteeing rights is to invest them in the individual, so that redress can be obtained in specific cases. Individual rights cannot be sufficient to protect people,

---

161 A. Weale (1983) *Political theory and social policy*, London: Macmillan.

162 See e.g. M.D.A. Freeman (1983) *The rights and wrongs of children*, London: Pinter; W. Stainton Rogers, D. Hevey and E. Ash (1989) *Child abuse and neglect*, London: Batsford.

163 See e.g. J.P. Martin (1985) *Hospitals in trouble*, Oxford: Blackwell.

because the rights are often difficult to exercise, but they are necessary; without them, people who are socially isolated are rendered powerless, and their circumstances are liable to be overlooked.

II.2.c.i Freedom is a precondition for well-being.

The assertion of liberty is generally accepted in modern society, which does not mean that it is unproblematic. Liberty means three things. First, it means freedom from constraint – the reaction against tyranny, the freedom to worship – and the freedom to proceed without obstacles, the 'career open to the talents'. Second, it means the power to act, the sense in which it was taken by socialists; people could not be free if they were incapacitated by hunger and disease, or if they were unable to act collectively. Third, it means psychological liberation – the ability to think for oneself. These three elements stand together as one: every freedom, MacCallum has argued, consists of freedom of a person from restraint to do something.[164]

All freedoms are not equal. Some freedoms, like freedom of religion or freedom of assembly, are more important than others, like the freedom to drive at a speed of one's choosing. Freedoms which protect people's welfare are important. They include, for example, the security of the person, the ability to associate with other people, the ability to form relationships with other people and the power to have and raise children.

The assertion that liberty is necessary for well-being is subject to the same reservation made more generally about rights: it is possible for a person not to be free and still to experience well-being. Liberty is not a guarantee of well-being. Indeed, in so far as liberty includes the power to make decisions which are destructive of a person's well-being, the argument can be made that liberty and welfare are unrelated.

The central argument against this is that people are not free to destroy their welfare. People are not free, in the name of freedom, to do things which diminish their freedom. Most obviously, they cannot sell themselves into slavery, and in many cases they can be prevented from committing suicide (which, like slavery, is a choice not to make any more choices). Welfare is necessary if people are to have the power to act, and a degree of psychological freedom is required if autonomous decisions are to be made.

II.2.c.ii Political protection is required to guarantee welfare.

Political conditions offer security or insecurity in another sense; the political framework determines the prospect of peace or war, the rights

---

164 G. MacCallum (1967) 'Negative and positive freedom', *Philosophical Review*, 76: 312–334.

of minorities, and the rule of law. As with other basic needs, the effect of a lack of security is liable to dominate every aspect of social relationships, and the power of political processes to threaten security makes this another precondition of welfare.

Unlike the other factors, political protection of this kind is primarily a negative condition; it is concerned with preventing things from happening, rather than ensuring that certain conditions are met. (There is, of course, an argument for governments to foster welfare more positively, but that is not a precondition for welfare; it will be considered later.)

II.2.c.iii   Economic and social rights are preconditions for well-being.

The absence of impediments to the pursuit of welfare is necessary to welfare, but it cannot be sufficient. T.H. Marshall distinguished three main kinds of rights: the civil rights of the eighteenth century, which guaranteed political protection; the economic rights of the nineteenth, which developed basic entitlements to material goods; and the social rights of the twentieth century, which have been used to develop systems of social protection.[165]

Economic and social rights, like civil rights, have both negative and positive meanings. In negative terms, actions should not be taken which directly impair people's well-being, and people should not be actively prevented from pursuing objectives which will further their well-being. In positive terms, there are economic and social components to well-being, and without them well-being cannot be achieved. The description of these components as 'rights' relates the process of achieving well-being directly to the people who experience it.

II.2.c.iv   Rights exist.

Saying that rights are essential is not the same as saying that they exist; it only asserts that they ought to exist. But rights do exist, and there are two processes by which they come into existence. One is through the obligations which people have acquired to each other in the course of everyday social interaction – the rights and duties of children, families and neighbours. If social interaction generates obligations, it also generates claim rights. Claim rights are only a form of obligation seen from a different perspective (▶ II.2.c). This depends on the structure of obligation – the social norms discussed in previous sections (▶ I.1.c). The bulk of rights provided through collective social action are particular rights, which relate to the obligations of specific individuals. Where people have paid

---

165 T.H. Marshall (1982) *The right to welfare*, London: Heinemann.

subscriptions or contributions for social insurance, they acquire a right to receive benefits. This is the dominant form of social welfare provision in continental Europe, and much of the world.

There are also, however, general rights – rights which are held, not by particular individuals, but by anyone who is in a category. People can have rights for diverse reasons – because they are old, sick, disabled, children, citizens of a country, or whatever. These rights, and the obligations which correspond to them, exist morally for the simple reason that people believe they exist; obligations are intersubjective, and if people believe that they are obliged, and act accordingly, they are obliged. (This, of course, leaves such rights open to challenge by anyone who wants to shout that the emperor has no clothes.)[166] There are examples of general obligations held by particular individuals – the rights of children are taken to impose obligations on parents[167] – but for the most part the obligations which correspond to general rights are held by society as a whole.

The name most often given to this constellation of rights is 'citizenship'. Although citizenship has a narrow, legal construction related to nationality, it also has two broader senses. Citizenship refers to the set of rights which a person enjoys, or the status which makes it possible to have rights.[168] More broadly still, citizenship is increasingly used in a social sense, to refer to membership of a society, and the pattern of general rights and obligations between people and the society which they are part of.[169] From the perspective of welfare, the concept of citizenship has significant limitations. First, the issue of citizenship is addressed to a specific type of general right; it is not concerned with the particular rights on which many systems of welfare principally depend. The issue has been important for the development of welfare provision in the United Kingdom, but the assumption that it must be equally important elsewhere is a parochial one. Second, the idea of citizenship is inherently exclusive as well as inclusive: it identifies some people as holding general rights while others do not. This reflects the reality of many rights and entitlements, but it does not exhaust the possibilities. There may also be general rights which do not depend on membership of a society, but extend to people regardless of their status. Some countries, including the UK and some states in the US, offer a (limited) range of

---

166 E.g. F. Hayek (1976) *Law, legislation and liberty*, vol. 2: *The mirage of social justice*, London: Routledge and Kegan Paul.

167 UN Declaration of the Rights of the Child.

168 R.E. Goodin (1982) *Political theory and public policy*, Chicago: University of Chicago Press, ch. 5.

169 G. Pascall (1993) 'Citizenship – a feminist analysis', in G. Drover and P. Kearns (1993) *New approaches to welfare theory*, Aldershot: Edward Elgar; A. Rees (1995) 'The promise of social citizenship', *Policy and Politics*, 23 (4): 313–325.

services to anyone within a category – in the UK, certain classes of health care, and in the US education for the children of illegal immigrants. This is a recognition of a range of rights and obligations that go beyond citizenship.

SOCIAL PROTECTION

II.3 Social protection is necessary to secure welfare.

Social protection
- II.3.a   *Social protection is necessary for welfare.*
- II.3.a.i   Social protection requires collective action.
- II.3.a.ii   Social protection is based in solidarity.
- II.3.a.iii   Social protection should be as comprehensive as possible.

The limits of the market
- II.3.b   *Markets are insufficient to guarantee welfare.*
- II.3.b.i   Solidaristic obligations do not guarantee comprehensive social protection.
- II.3.b.ii   Markets are liable to exclude those in need.
- II.3.b.iii   Markets may also have undesirable social effects.

The social services
- II.3.c   *Social protection requires social services.*
- II.3.c.i   Social services provide welfare.
- II.3.c.ii   Social services do not have to be provided through collective action.
- II.3.c.iii   Social services develop in a social context.

The moral basis of welfare provision
- II.3.d   *Social protection, and social services, are moral activities.*
- II.3.d.i   Collective action for welfare is morally informed.
- II.3.d.ii   Collective action is subject to moral conflicts.

Social protection

II.3.a Social protection is necessary for welfare.

The idea of 'social protection' generally embraces both the principle of collective action to cover a range of contingencies, and the provision of services to deal with needs – because the existence of such services is part of offering security. Social protection is necessary for welfare, both because it provides for needs which impair welfare, and because without it people become insecure.

Although social protection is necessary for welfare, it is far from sufficient. From the preceding sections, it is clear that the conditions for welfare include the satisfaction of physical and material needs, the scope to satisfy aspirations, social and economic rights, basic security and economic development. Social protection is a necessary means of securing what is there; it is not an adequate substitute for what is not.

II.3.a.i   Social protection requires collective action.

Social protection depends on collective action. This is because social protection has the characteristics of solidarity – the recognition of mutual responsibility (▸ I.3.a) – and pooled risk, where responsibility for the risks of one person is accepted by others (▸ I.3.b). Even if, in principle, measures for social protection could be instigated by people in need themselves, in practice it is often impossible for them to do so, because the conditions in which they may need protection – including poverty, physical incapacity, mental impairment and destitution – are conditions which also prevent people from acting. Effective social protection demands the contribution of other people in society, who are not themselves in need at the same time.

II.3.a.ii   Social protection is based in solidarity.

The central principle of social protection is solidarity, in the sense of obligations to others (▸ I.3.a). The basic principle is simple enough: that when a member of a society experiences a contingency in which support is deemed to be required, or moves into a recognized 'state of dependency' like childhood or old age, an obligation to that person will exist.[170]

In its earliest manifestations, social protection was seen as a form of charity. Charity is a distinctive form of social solidarity, in which obligations are recognized, but the obligations are not held to the recipient. One motivation is religious: the primary obligation is to God. Another is communal: the obligation is to the community in general. Charity, then, provides a degree of protection without granting correlative rights.

Although the charitable motive has survived, the organization of social protection has shifted towards a foundation in the principles of mutual

---

170 The term 'state of dependency' is from R. Titmuss (1963) *Essays on the welfare state*, London: Allen and Unwin, p. 42.

aid. The central principle of social protection is the pooling of risk. In mutual aid insurance, people pay a premium in order to protect themselves against certain contingencies. This places social protection more directly on the basis of reciprocal obligation. This form of social protection is often supplemented by commercial arrangements, which have duplicated the pattern of formal mutual aid.

A third form of solidarity, which has become increasingly important in the course of the twentieth century, is the growth of mutual obligation to others on the basis of membership of a society. This is an explicit part of the rationale for the development of solidarity in French social policy;[171] measures like the Fonds National de Solidarité for elderly people who have never worked are based on the idea of shared responsibility for everyone in France. This means that the principle of solidarity, initially focused on mutual aid, has come to stand for measures which rely on redistribution.

II.3.a.iii   Social protection should be as comprehensive as possible.

The nature of social protection is that it covers, not just need, but risk – the possibility that needs may arise. It is perfectly possible for formal arrangements for social protection to cover only a privileged minority: Ferrera characterizes social protection systems in Southern Europe as polarized, with a sharply defined dualism distinguishing those who are best protected from others.[172] But this is equivalent to a lack of protection for others.

Services in many countries are not universal. The Bismarckian system of provision in Germany is based on pooled risks only for those below a set income; those on higher incomes (roughly the top 20 per cent) are supposed to be able to make their own arrangements. On the face of the matter, this seems to contradict the proposition which is considered here, that protection needs to be comprehensive. But the basic argument for social protection is not that everyone should be encompassed within the same system, but that each person needs to be protected against eventualities. This can be achieved in many ways, and there are arguments for flexibility. It should perhaps be noted that the coverage of the German system is less than complete, but complementary strategies can be adopted to develop general coverage.

The absence of social protection is not a failure of welfare in itself, because those who are not covered are not necessarily in need. It becomes a failure of welfare only when people are left with needs unmet

---

171 J-J. Dupeyroux (1998) *Droit de la sécurité sociale*, Paris: Dalloz, p. 290.

172 M. Ferrera (1996) 'The "Southern Model" of welfare in social Europe', *Journal of European Social Policy*, 6 (1): 17–37.

as a result of the lack of cover, or when others become insecure as a consequence. As coverage becomes more widespread, the risk that a person in need will not be provided for reduces. This has justified a process of 'generalization' – the idea comes from France[173] – to extend the scope of solidarity to the greatest possible extent. It has led, too, in several countries to the progressive universalization of social protection, particularly for health care;[174] people wish to be covered. It is striking that it is in the Nordic countries, where voluntary mutual aid has been most developed, that the principle of universalism is also strongest.

This falls short, perhaps, of a case for full universal coverage, but it leads in a similar direction. The purpose of extending social protection is to reduce the area of risk. As long as the marginal risk is not negligible, the argument for extending coverage continues to apply. Other arguments add further weight to the case for extension – notably, arguments based in citizenship and rights (► II.2.c.iv). This means that although social protection may not be truly comprehensive, it will grow to be as comprehensive as possible in particular circumstances.

The limits of the market

II.3.b   Markets are insufficient to guarantee welfare.

Conventionally, the production of welfare provision by a range of independent actors is referred to as a 'market'. It is not a market in the sense in which that term is used in economic theory: many of the actors are charitable, mutualist or non-profit organizations, and even those who have a profit-making function may, like private hospitals in the US or building societies in the UK, retain some of the aspirations or orientation of the voluntary sector.

The patterns of solidarity through which social protection is provided in such a market are complex, and the mechanisms which exist for social protection are extensive. There are still, however, important limitations on the scope of social protection on this basis. In some cases, people may be excluded, or left out. In others, even where networks of solidarity exist, the level of protection which is provided may not be adequate to cover the circumstances of the person in need.

Note that this is not what economists call 'market failure'. Market failure is a characteristic of developed economic markets in which goods are exchanged through the price mechanism. It happens principally

---

173 Dupeyroux (1998).

174 Organization for Economic Cooperation and Development (1990) *Health care systems in transition*, Paris: OECD; OECD (1992) *The reform of health care*, Paris: OECD.

when prices fail to convey the appropriate signals about costs and benefits (for example, when markets are distorted by monopolistic production or when there are social aspects of a decision).[175] Commercial markets have a limited relevance to welfare and social protection – their methods and objectives are different. If a commercial market fails, there may also be a failure of welfare, but the positions are not equivalent: people can suffer when the market is working well, and manage even when it is working inefficiently. The kind of failure which is being pointed to here is much more fundamental: markets do not, and cannot, guarantee welfare for all the population.

II.3.b.i   Solidaristic obligations do not guarantee comprehensive social protection.

Social protection calls for more than a vague commitment from members of a society to support each other. The networks of social obligation which exist are certainly sufficient to provide support for some people; the clearest example of this are children in families, who in normal circumstances, in most societies, will receive support whether or not there are formal rules or structures to guarantee their position. But, by the same token, there are many people who are not adequately protected. Most obviously, there are people without families – children who are orphaned or abandoned, like the street children of South America, and old people who have outlived the people who might have supported them. There are networks in which obligations have failed or been repudiated – such as families in which parents neglect or deny children, children repudiate their aged parents. Then there are those who have networks of support, but where there are insufficient resources within that network to meet their needs. One of the principal causes of low income in developed countries is long-term sickness or disability, which affects not only the people who experience it but also the people who have to look after them, or who might otherwise have depended on them. The extent to which people are covered by networks of solidarity is intermittent, and social protection requires more than such networks generate spontaneously.

The main limitation of this system is the tendency to exclude people in greatest need, through 'adverse selection'. People in the greatest need represent the greatest liability; the effect of accepting these liabilities is to increase costs. It is in the interests of others who have pooled risks to avoid excessive liabilities. The same principle applies to commercial transactions. Even when the primary motivation of an insurer is mutualist, there is a pressure to exclude bad risks. A mutual aid society which does not select will have greater costs, and higher subscriptions, than one

---

175 S.J. Bailey (1995) *Public sector economics*, Basingstoke: Macmillan, pp. 26–38.

which does. If individuals with lower needs default, in order to pay lower subscriptions, costs rise further. This can only be countered by excluding high risks, or by making policy holders bear a higher proportion of the risks themselves. 'Let's face it', in the words of one insurer: 'competition in health care is all about making sure you don't have ill people on your books'.[176]

The second problem is the problem of 'moral hazard': that some people bring their conditions on themselves. People who smoke, or who are involved in dangerous sports, are voluntarily exposing themselves to risk, and in situations where risks are pooled this imposes a liability on others. The effect of moral hazard is greatly to reduce the power of solidaristic obligation; many people consider that it exempts them from obligation altogether. Exclusion, however, leaves some people without cover, which jeopardizes their welfare.

II.3.b.ii   Markets are liable to exclude those in need.

If a market is based on a range of services provided under different terms, the test of the market is how far the system as a whole offers the necessary degree of social protection. Commercial services offer supplementary provision to that of mutual aid, but in many areas of welfare provision their scope is limited; the dominant model in the provision of health care and social security is mutualist. By contrast, the private sector is extensively involved in housing provision and personal services like cleaning, cooking and physical assistance.

The most basic problem, which applies both to commercial transactions and to patterns of mutual aid, is that individuals have to be able either to pay for services, or to pay the premium in order to be covered. This presumes a stable economic position. Advocates of market-based provision have generally taken this to be an argument about the distribution of resources, rather than about the character of the market itself; and the issue of distribution, Seldon argues, is separable in principle from the mechanism which is appropriate to deliver services. Where people are short of food, few commentators would argue for a social service to provide it; rather, the argument is made for social security provision to give people the money to buy it.[177] But even where people do have the money, there may still be problems of exclusion: from the point of view of social protection and coverage, the problems of adverse selection and moral hazard continue to apply, and in commercial services they are not mitigated to the same extent as in the voluntary sector by the acceptance of continuing moral responsibilities.

---

176 Cited in H. Glennerster (1997) *Paying for welfare: towards 2000*, Hemel Hempstead: Prentice-Hall, p. 22.
177 A. Seldon (1977) *Charge!* London: Temple Smith.

II.3.b.iii   Markets may also have undesirable social effects.

There are well-documented problems in the provision of social protection through markets. Most relate to limitations in coverage, but there are also arguments about the efficiency of markets. The private and voluntary sectors misallocate resources geographically, encouraging concentration of resources rather than dispersion.[178] They duplicate resources, because duplication is necessary to competition. In some cases, notably in the provision of health care, markets encourage over-consumption. These arguments cannot, however, be decided only as matters of general principle; there are circumstances in which the private market operates efficiently and effectively (for example, food distribution), and others in which its performance is much more questionable (such as health care). The arguments need to be considered case by case.

Markets also have social implications beyond the interests of the people who engage in them. One problem, which is widely recognized in the economic literature, is the problem of externalities: the actions of people engaged in a transaction may affect others who are not otherwise involved. Decisions about education, health and work affect other people, and a society as a whole. A further problem, which is not so widely recognized, is that legitimate individual decisions can lead to social problems. A risk of 1 in 1,000 is small for an individual – there are much greater risks in smoking, pregnancy, motorcycling and so forth – but in a society of 200 million people it will affect 200,000 of them. This general point overlaps with a third issue. Social priorities, and obligations, may be different from the aggregated effects of personal choices; issues like the education of children, the housing of the workforce or the health of old people have often, for that reason, been the focus of remedial collective action. This argument is described in the economic literature as a problem of 'merit goods' – goods and services which are worth more to society than they appear to be worth when left to individual decisions.[179]

The social services

II.3.c   Social protection requires social services.

Social services are organized or institutional forms of service delivery. They can be provided in several ways – including, in the terms discussed so far, charitable provision, mutual aid, non-profit, unpaid

---

178 R. Pahl (1975) *Whose city?* Harmondsworth: Penguin; K. Jones, J. Brown and J. Bradshaw (1978) *Issues in social policy*, London: Routledge and Kegan Paul, ch. 5.

179 Bailey (1995), ch. 2.

and private services. They are defined, not by the principle on which they are organized, but by the way in which they respond to need. Social services are services: they do things for people, like providing them with help, advice or personal care. They are services for people in need; the distinguishing characteristic of social services, as opposed to public services, is that they address issues which are liable to make people dependent on others – issues like sickness, old age, disability or unemployment.

It may not be immediately obvious why social services should be favoured over any other method of providing social protection. Some contingencies can be dealt with without any form of institutional service delivery. If people are unable to feed themselves, the argument is not usually made for a food service which will grow, prepare and deliver their food; it is for financial assistance which will enable them to buy the food they need. The same arguments can be made for the provision of essential needs, including food, water, fuel and health care.

There are, however, certain circumstances in which the provision of financial assistance cannot cover the needs. An example is the situation of people who lack the capacity to make decisions. Young children or people with mental disorders may not be able to undertake the measures necessary to obtain necessary care or services. The same applies to certain conditions which interfere directly with the ability of people to commission and direct the services they receive. An example might be the victims of traffic accidents: people who have just been run over are not always at their best, and they may find it difficult to negotiate the terms of their treatment.

Beyond this, there are many services that people find it difficult to commission for themselves. It is possible to build a house commercially by approaching a sequence of specialized workers, but few people do so; they buy the services of a builder or architect, who will subcontract the work for them. When people buy health services, residential care, or education for their children, they commonly buy a whole service, rather than bits of services. For much the same reasons when these kinds of services have been commissioned by solidaristic mutual aid or insurance organizations, they have often bought services, rather than distributing cash for members to buy the services themselves.

The basic social services are conventionally understood as health care; social care (help with personal needs, either in people's own homes or in residential settings); education; social housing; and social security. (Social security, or income maintenance, can equally be seen as an alternative to social services; it represents the provision of finance to meet needs, rather than an organized response to the need itself.) These are the 'big five', but many other services might be included: for example, counselling, employment services, and transport might be seen in a similar light. Equally, wherever services are provided in place of market facilities – such as the provision of food, clothing, fuel or furniture – these services are seen as aspects of social services.

Social services have developed, not because they are the only means by which needs can be met, but because they are appropriate to the kinds of needs which social protection covers. The precise kinds of service, and the conditions under which they are offered, depend on circumstances, and in particular on what alternative forms of provision exist. It seems unavoidable, though, that some kind of social service will be required.

II.3.c.i Social services provide welfare.

If welfare depends on more than needs, it requires more than a guarantee against needs to protect people's welfare. The role of social services extends beyond social protection itself, and the functions of social services include not only responses to need, but a range of other activities concerned with the promotion of welfare. The most important of these are facilitative and developmental functions. Social services facilitate welfare by providing services to help people to help themselves, or bringing them in contact with others: for example, offering education, giving advice or providing information (like an employment exchange). The developmental functions are concerned with enabling people: the most important is education, though services for health, employment and social work may have similar aims.

II.3.c.ii Social services do not have to be provided through collective action.

Social services have always been characterized by collective action. Many of the earliest welfare services – schools, orphanages, hospices and so forth – were voluntary or charitable in nature. Collective action by mutual aid societies also tended to develop in situations where there were few, or no, alternatives. Commercial organizations for profit, by contrast, have had a relatively limited role in this field, because profits are rarely maximized through focusing on people with considerable needs but limited resources. Collectively based social services developed because the protection they provided was needed, and it was not provided through the private sector.

Despite this trend, it is not necessary for the organization and delivery of services to be done collectively, and in practice social services may be provided in a range of different ways, including commercial provision. Most obviously, insurance cover is collective (because it involves the pooling of risk) but the financial payments from insurance can be used in the market. There is, then, a clear distinction to be made between the principle of social protection and the provision of social services. Social protection has to be collective (▸ II.3.a.i); social services do not.

II.3.c.iii   *Social services develop in a social context.*

There is a view that the development of social protection has depended primarily on the interaction of factors in industrial society.[180] If social protection depends on a structure of interdependency, solidarity and social obligation, it cannot be mainly attributable to the process of industrialization, because these characteristics are not confined to economically developed societies. Social protection must occur in undeveloped societies as well as developed ones. This is indeed the case; Sahlins reviews anthropological evidence of the application of solidarity in a wide range of tribal societies.[181] Economic development has a direct effect on this process – a combination of interdependency, and the creation of the means by which welfare can be increased (▸ II.2.a) – but it is not sufficient to explain the establishment of social protection.

Industrial society shapes the specific forms which social protection takes in practice. Social services have developed in the society of which they are part, and the form they take reflects the conditions in that society. The forum around which many welfare organizations have been built is the workplace, with an emphasis either on the role of the unions, or the employer, or both, depending on the conditions at the time. (This is true, in different ways, both in Europe and Japan.)[182] Religious organizations have played a major part: the 'pillarization' of social services in the Netherlands was based on the distinction between Catholic, Protestant and secular organizations.[183] In other countries, welfare was built around such formal organizations as existed – in much of England, the Poor Law. (The arrangement in England was more complex: prior to the development of Poor Law services, the main administrative authority was held by magistrates.[184] The local gentry often had, in consequence, the threefold role of employer, giver of charity and exerciser of authority, and the response to poverty might fall into any of these categories.)

There is no simple formula to explain which social groupings are likely to be influential, and which will not. However, once a pattern of provision is established, any new initiative or development has to negotiate its role with the services which have already been developed. One way

---

180 G. Rimlinger (1971) *Welfare policy and industrialisation in Europe, America and Russia*, New York: John Wiley.

181 M. Sahlins (1974) *Stone age economics*, London: Tavistock.

182 Baldwin (1990); A. Gould (1993) *Capitalist welfare systems*, London: Longman, Pt 1; G. Esping-Andersen (1996) 'Hybrid or unique?: the Japanese welfare state between Europe and America', *Journal of European Social Policy*, 7 (3): 179–189.

183 M. Brenton (1982) 'Changing relationships in Dutch social services', *Journal of Social Policy*, 11 (1): 59–80.

184 S. Webb and B. Webb (1927) *English local government: the old Poor Law*, London: Cass.

of representing this process is, of course, historical: the idea of 'path dependency' has been used to explain how, once certain decisions about development have been made, systems come to develop along specific lines.[185] Historical explanations have an advantage over sociological ones; they take into account influences which have little to do with social factors – notably, in Europe, the effect of war and invasion. Whatever the mode of explanation, the central point is that welfare does not appear in a society from out of nowhere; it grows and develops on the basis of what is there.

The moral basis of welfare provision

II.3.d Social protection, and social services, are moral activities.

The idea that social protection and social services are moral activities should, by this stage of the argument, be unsurprising; social action is conditioned by moral norms, and the provision of welfare is no exception. But the provision of welfare is more deeply embedded in morality than many other activities. For one thing, the provision of welfare is required morally; there are obligations of solidarity which bind people to mutual support (▶ I.3.a). It is not just moral activity – there are good reasons of self-interest to go along with it – but it is inevitably moral in its nature. For another, welfare itself is an evaluative concept, which can only really be understood normatively. Where moral codes are not complied with, welfare is vitiated.

II.3.d.i Collective action for welfare is morally informed.

Whether people offer social protection to each other, or whether they band together specifically for the purpose of mutual aid, the action is morally informed. People are doing something which benefits them, and which they know to be right. This is a powerful combination.

This means not only that people are acting morally, but that they know that moral obligation is at issue. This has important consequences for the arrangements. People in such arrangements are sensitive, not just to moral obligation, but to immorality, which is another facet of morality. One of the few things which can wipe out a reciprocal moral obligation is the breach of moral obligation on the other side. In the view of many people, the effect of criminal activity, or fraud relating to welfare provision, is to extinguish their moral responsibility. This cannot be said with confidence, because there are other sources of duty besides mutual

---

185 D. Wilsford (1995) 'Path dependency, or why history makes it difficult but not impossible to reform health care systems in a big way', *Journal of Public Policy*, 14 (3): 251–283.

obligation: there are duties to other members of a community, and to humanity in general, which continue to apply whatever someone does.

II.3.d.ii *Collective action is subject to moral conflicts.*

Although there are general moral obligations to engage in collective action and mutual aid, these are not the only moral obligations which people have. There is clearly a strong potential for moral conflict. People have duties which come from their contact with others. For example, an obligation to pay a debt might be in conflict with obligations to one's family, and prior obligations are a common reason for default. This is not a good excuse, because both obligations continue to exist, even though they may be contradictory. Equally, there may be conflicts between the obligations of mutual aid and other moral codes (like political or religious beliefs). The value of freedom is often represented as if it was opposed to welfare, and individualism is opposed to communal values. But people can hold these ideas and values simultaneously; in many cases the positions can be reconciled, but even if they cannot, the choices people make do not have to be consistent.

II.4

WELFARE AND REDISTRIBUTION

II.4 Welfare implies redistribution.

Welfare in society
II.4.a	*The provision of welfare reflects the values of the society in which it takes place.*
II.4.a.i	Neutral actions can have biased consequences.
II.4.a.i(1)	Action which takes account of social conditions can reinforce them.
II.4.a.i(2)	Action which fails to take account of social conditions is liable to be inequitable.
II.4.a.ii	There are no neutral outcomes.

Social justice
II.4.b	*Social justice is a distributive principle.*
II.4.b.i	The principle of justice is a principle of consistency.
II.4.b.ii	Justice is not welfare.

Inequality
II.4.c	*Welfare is limited by social disadvantage.*
II.4.c.i	Inequality is disadvantage in a social context.
II.4.c.ii	The structure of social relationships implies disadvantage.
II.4.c.iii	Justice begins with equality.
II.4.c.iv	Inequalities which are not justifiable must be redressed.

Redistribution
II.4.d	*Social protection is redistributive.*
II.4.d.i	Redistribution is intrinsic to solidarity.
II.4.d.ii	The distribution of resources is a matter of convention.
II.4.d.iii	Redistribution is part of the rules of the game.

Redistribution between societies

II.4.e	*There are related obligations to people in other countries.*
II.4.e.i	Justice, equality and redistribution are only applied in specific social contexts.
II.4.e.ii	The scope of obligations to people in other countries is limited.

Welfare in society

II.4.a   The provision of welfare reflects the values of the society in which it takes place.

The provision of welfare is a moral activity (► II.3.d), and the values it enshrines are the values of the society it operates in. If a society values family ties, industrial production and national culture, welfare has to be expected to do the same.[186] (This is not to say that a society should value these things, or that it will be a better society if it does: 'work, family, country' was the slogan of Vichy France.) Although it is fairly obvious that collective action for welfare can develop new forms of social relationship in its own right, it often begins from existing social relationships: obligations relating to community, religious grouping or the workplace. Collective action for welfare may alter social relationships – perhaps reinforcing them, perhaps reducing their strength – but it is not very plausible to suppose that such arrangements are designed to change society fundamentally. Collective action is part of society: it begins as part of social relationships, and it continues as part of those relationships (► I.3.b.iv).

This also means, perhaps paradoxically, that the provision of welfare tends to be relatively little concerned with many key social issues, because these issues are taken for granted. Gender, family, sexuality and race have come in recent years to dominate the agenda for discussion in the study of social policy. In the study of social relationships, these issues are immensely important, and sociologists who have turned their attention to welfare have sought to find this importance reflected in the agenda of social protection. In many cases, however, the issues for policy are obscure, and a great deal of work has had to be devoted to making them visible.

II.4.a.i   *Neutral actions can have biased consequences.*

A neutral action is one which does not seek to change the conditions in which it is applied. Neutrality is important for fairness: in a neutral

---

186 F. Williams (1989) *Social policy: a critical introduction*, Cambridge: Polity.

process, there should be no bias, prejudice or favour. A neutral process does not, of course, necessarily produce a neutral outcome. A lottery is a neutral process: each ticket has an equal chance of winning. But people with more money can buy more tickets than people with less, so that winners are more likely to be better off. This is a simple illustration, but its effects are replicated again and again in social policy. In situations where people are disadvantaged, arrangements which fail to remove disadvantage may give the appearance of perpetuating it. Women tend to receive less than men for jobs of apparently similar value. (I write 'apparently' because there is a high degree of segregation between the sexes, and there is no clear yardstick by which value can be established. Since many of the lowest paid jobs are more important for society than many of the highest, the idea of 'equal value' is problematic.) A system of social protection which reflects the pay of workers will pay less to women. The origins of this inequality lie in the pay structure, not the system of social protection, but it is a common criticism of social protection systems that they maintain gender inequality.

The structure of society is unequal (▸ I.2.c.i), and the effect of social protection in an unequal society is often to produce unequal consequences. There is a general problem relating to financial compensation, that the value of an item is likely to reflect the valuation which the market places on it, and the market is subject to the wishes of people who have resources. Compensation for loss of earnings is worth more to the person who earns more. Compensation for personal injury tends to reflect the structure of salaries, which in turn reflects the structure of inequality. Compensation for property suffers from the same problems: a house which is worth ten times more than the average is unlikely to be ten times more house; the valuation reflects the willingness and ability of a minor part of the market to pay for its facilities or special characteristics. Accepting cash valuations has the further effect of saying that the house of a richer person matters ten times more than the house of a poor one: when railways were built through towns, they went through the areas populated by poorer people, because that was the economic way to develop.

The provision of welfare is liable to reflect the structure of a society, then, unless specific measures are taken to prevent it. Criticisms of welfare as 'gendered', or of 'institutional racism' in welfare states, are based in the argument that welfare provision systematically produces disadvantage for women and racial minorities. There are cases of explicit discrimination, but in modern times they have become exceptional; the substance of the complaint is not primarily that discrimination is done directly, but that it is done in effect. The inadequacy of community care services becomes a problem for women, because it is women, in practice, who do most of the caring.[187] The housing conditions of racial minorities

---

187 C. Ungerson (ed.) (1990) *Gender and caring*, Hemel Hempstead: Harvester Wheatsheaf.

show the effects of cumulative disadvantage through a series of social and administrative processes.[188]

In an unequal society, an apparently neutral measure will not redress, and may replicate, the disadvantage these groups experience. This is primarily a criticism of society, rather than welfare provision; it condemns welfare provision for failing to change situations it was never designed to change. That is not an excuse, because it is perfectly legitimate to argue that welfare should have been designed to change these things. It needs to be understood, however, that the point is directed at social conditions, rather than being a fundamental criticism of welfare.

II.4.a.i(1)   Action which takes account of social conditions can reinforce them.

The assumptions made about social relationships can affect the pattern of welfare provision, and with it the impact of social protection on society. A social protection system which makes allowance for dependants, for example, has to define who is, and who is not, entitled to receive protection. In a society where the dominant norm is that of a male breadwinner with a dependent wife, the effect of specifying that only a 'wife' may receive an allowance is potentially discriminatory; it means that women with dependent husbands may not be covered. The effect of specifying a 'spouse' does not discriminate on the basis of gender, but does discriminate between those who are married and those who are not. More recently, there have been complaints that same-sex partners are not recognized as dependants. The arguments are muddled: a sexual relationship, or a personal commitment, is distinct from the issue of dependency. What matters is the common use of resources in a household. Unconnected issues have been lumped together because of the (equally questionable) assumptions about matrimony.

One curious side-effect of such assumptions is that systems can become a reward for conformity. People who are married receive rewards that unmarried people do not; nuclear families are protected when extended families may not be. At the same time, there may be perverse results. 'Cohabitation rules' are based on the principle that married couples should not be treated worse than unmarried couples, so that an unmarried couple have their resources aggregated in the same way. The effect is also, however, to penalize unmarried fathers for accepting responsibility for a child.

---

188 J. Rex (1988) 'Race and the urban system', in *The ghetto and the underclass*, Aldershot: Avebury; S.J. Smith (1989) *The politics of 'race' and residence*, Cambridge: Polity.

Although some authors are vehement about the effects of such 'incentives',[189] there is very little evidence to show that people's behaviour is greatly altered by rewards or penalties of this sort.[190] As a moral issue, though, there is evident concern that distributive measures should not punish people for doing what is right, or reward them for doing what is wrong. In so far as the conditions of social protection reflect existing circumstances, they might seem to convey approval; and since social protection is concerned with conditions which are undesirable, like disability, unemployment and poverty, the accusation is often made that it is aggravating the conditions it is designed to help.[191]

II.4.a.i(2) Action which fails to take account of social conditions is liable to be inequitable.

The main way to avoid this kind of effect is to ignore social conditions – to begin with a presumption of equality and to treat people on an equivalent basis. The problem with this is that it leads to inequity, sometimes seriously so. If married people were to be treated as individuals, rather than as members of a household unit, the effect would be greatly to enhance the position of non-working spouses, including non-working spouses in relatively rich households. The rules for aggregation of household resources are intended to prevent that. Similarly, the effect of disaggregating the resources of students in higher education from their parents has been to favour richer families of higher status. It is possible, then, to avoid reinforcing existing conditions, but the results are not certain to be satisfactory.

II.4.a.ii There are no neutral outcomes.

If neutral actions have biased consequences, the only way to achieve an unbiased outcome is to select a means of addressing the issues which is not neutral, but designed to produce a different balance. The only cases in which neutral outcomes can be achieved are where people begin from a position of equality. This is the position in courts of law, which begin from the proposition that everyone is equal before the law; in principle, legal neutrality is possible, even if it is difficult to achieve in practice. In theory, too, many societies are committed to the equality of their members, though because not everyone is equally able to participate in such societies, the effect is not neutral in social terms. In the field of welfare provision, there are no neutral outcomes.

---

189 E.g. C. Murray (1984) *Losing ground*, New York: Basic Books.

190 See e.g. J. Pechman and M. Timpane (1975) *Work incentives and income guarantees*, Washington: Brookings, which describes a controlled experiment.

191 H. Spencer (1851) *Social statics*, London: Murray, 1984.

Social justice

II.4.b   Social justice is a distributive principle.

Justice is used in two main senses. The Platonic use of the term represents justice as what is morally right, or good.[192] The Aristotelian use sees justice as a distributive term, closely associated with fairness. The just, Aristotle wrote, is the proportionate.[193] Corrective justice, or criminal justice, is done by treating someone proportionately to their offence. Distributive justice demands an allocation between people which is proportionate to certain criteria, such as their needs, their desert, or their rights. In both senses of the term, social justice can act as a distributive principle, governing the allocation of resources in a society.

II.4.b.i   *The principle of justice is a principle of consistency.*

The basic argument for justice is an argument for consistency. If two people have committed the same crime, they should be treated similarly. Injustice occurs when factors are taken into account which are irrelevant; the fact that one person is a gypsy, or another happens to be related to the local magistrate, should not influence the decision unless it is directly germane to the case. Conversely, if two people have committed different offences, they should not be treated in the same way. The same principle applies in distributive justice: like cases are treated alike, and different cases differently.

II.4.b.ii   *Justice is not welfare.*

Social justice and welfare are not equivalent principles, and there may be cases in which justice leads to a reduction in welfare. This is most obviously true of the concept of corrective justice, which argues that in some cases it is appropriate to punish people and so to make them worse off. Distributive justice means that if the welfare of some people is reduced, the welfare of others is increased.

It is possible to argue that redistribution can lead to an increase in welfare overall. The basic economic argument is that income and wealth have a diminishing marginal utility – £1 is worth less to a richer person than to a poorer one. The net effect of redistribution is therefore to increase the total sum of welfare.[194] This argument is based on the assumption that the utility refers to the same kind of spending, on the

---

192 Plato, *The republic*, in R. Hare and D. Russell (eds) *The dialogues of Plato: volume 4*, London: Sphere, 1970.

193 Aristotle, *Ethics*, ed. J. Thomson, Harmondsworth: Penguin, 1953.

194 A. Pigou (1932) *The economics of welfare*, London: Macmillan, p. 89.

same kinds of needs. Basic needs are important at lower levels of income, but other needs become evident at higher levels of income; achieving personal goals and ambitions also matter (▸ II.1.a.iii). The implication is not that welfare overall is increased by the transfer, but that one kind of welfare should be sacrificed in order to foster another. That is a tenable position, and one for which I have much sympathy – it is argued by everyone who advocates the transfer of resources from developed economies to poor, less developed economies – but it would be mistaken to assume that it involves no real sacrifice on the part of the richer person.

Inequality

II.4.c   Welfare is limited by social disadvantage.

Poverty, or the denial of welfare, is founded in social relationships as much as it is in material circumstances (▸ II.1.b.i). One effect of disadvantage in social relationships is a lessening of the quality of relationships in itself. People who have inferior status have not only limited access to social resources and opportunities, but a diminished set of social responsibilities (▸ I.2.c.i). Their integration into society, and their solidarity with others, is reduced. At the same time, disadvantage in social relationships reduces entitlements, and so the power that people have to command resources. The link between low status and low economic position is not coincidental.

People can maintain their welfare, even if they are unequal; disadvantage alone does not mean that material circumstances are unsatisfactory, or that security is threatened. But disadvantage is clearly related to unsatisfactory circumstances, and the more extreme the disadvantage, the more likely it is that welfare will be vitiated.

This might imply that welfare is diminished in proportion to disadvantage, so that as disadvantage increases, welfare diminishes. This view is tenable, but the alternative, more prevalent, view is that there is some point or threshold at which the disadvantage becomes crucial, and disadvantage leads directly to deprivation.[195] This perception is central to the argument that distributive justice can increase welfare. If welfare is based on the sum of utilities in a society, the argument for the redistribution of income is thin. If, on the other hand, one believes that a primary objective of social protection should be the avoidance of suffering, the existence of a threshold of suffering makes it possible to define both the objectives and the limits of redistribution: people have to be brought above that threshold.

---

195 D. Gordon and C. Pantazis (eds) (1997) *Breadline Britain in the 1990s*, Aldershot: Ashgate.

II.4.c.i *Inequality is disadvantage in a social context.*

Social inequality occurs whenever people are disadvantaged relative to others in a society. To say that someone is disadvantaged is not just to say that they are in a less desirable position than others; I would like to be able to play the piano, but I cannot say that I am disadvantaged because I can't. A person who has a chronic respiratory illness is clearly worse off than another person who does not, but is not necessarily 'disadvantaged' in relation to the other person. Two people in different states of health might, however, be advantaged or disadvantaged relative to each other if, for example, they were in competition for a job, or for different levels of health care. Disadvantage is based on some kind of social relationship, or common social element. Inequality is disadvantage which is general, rather than specific to certain circumstances.

Inequality is not just difference. People are different in many ways: they can be tall or short, thin or fat, old or young, and so forth. These differences imply inequality only if the difference leads to disadvantage. Many differences can cause disadvantage in social relationships. Differences of gender, 'race' or age commonly lead to discrimination and differential opportunities. Those who are opposed to inequality are not opposed to difference; no one argues that men and women should become asexual, or that everyone should be the same age. They are opposed to the social disadvantage which stems from difference, not the difference itself.

Some differences, however, are not true differences at all, but simple descriptions of disadvantage. Money is a form of entitlement – a unit of exchange, which allows command over resources. Having a different amount of money from another person means, in its very nature, that the person with more has a greater command over resources than the person with less. In a competition for scarce resources, it is the person with more money who will obtain them. Having low income and wealth is, then, a form of disadvantage, and inequality of income is an important form of inequality.

II.4.c.ii *The structure of social relationships implies disadvantage.*

Some element of disadvantage is implicit in social relationships. Social roles are highly differentiated, which is fundamental to interdependence, and these differences are associated with a range of differential rights and obligations (▸ I.2.c.i). Charvet argues, on that basis, that inequality is an integral element of any complex society.[196] I think this has to be right.

---

196 J. Charvet (1983) 'The idea of equality as a substantive principle of society', in W. Letwin (ed.) *Against equality*, London: Macmillan.

This does not, however, mean that disadvantage must just be accepted: inequality can create serious problems for social integration, and so for a society; too much inequality creates a social distance which prevents people from interacting with each other. Many commentators have sought to account for the source of disadvantage in the structure of class or power relations,[197] but for the most part the phenomena they are trying to explain need no explanation. Without corrective action, the effects of inequality are liable to be reproduced in subsequent allocations of resources (▶ II.4.a.ii), and such corrective action is only likely to be taken if there is some mechanism through which disadvantage can be remedied. The main role of concepts like class or power is to explain how movements for change can be passed over or defused.

II.4.c.iii Justice begins with equality.

The principle of justice is a principle of proportionality, not of equality. People who meet different criteria are not treated equivalently; we should not want everyone who comes to trial to receive the same punishment, irrespective of criteria such as guilt or the nature of the offence, and most of us would not want everyone to receive the same income, irrespective of their needs, the value of their contribution to society, the character of their work.

Justice does, however, contain a presumption of equality. If people are treated consistently, and there are no reasons to distinguish between them, then any distribution will in the first instance be an equal distribution. Inequalities have to be justified by relevant criteria.

II.4.c.iv Inequalities which are not justifiable must be redressed.

Inequalities can be justified in several ways, but it is difficult to justify them by their effect on welfare. Rawls suggests that inequality is justifiable if it leads to people at the bottom being made better off.[198] Rawls has been criticized for ignoring the importance of structured social disadvantage. His mistake is to consider welfare in terms of absolute resources, without considering its relational components.[199] If the implication of disadvantage is that a person achieves material improvements at the expense of social exclusion (the position of the domestic slave in ancient Greece or Rome), it may not be acceptable.

---

197 Two of the most influential are F. Engels (1934) *Anti-Dühring*, London: Lawrence and Wishart, and M. Foucault (1976) *Histoire de la sexualité: la volonté de savoir*, Paris: Gallimard.

198 J. Rawls (1971) *A theory of justice*, Oxford: Oxford University Press.

199 N. Daniels (1975) *Reading Rawls*, Oxford: Blackwell.

There may well be disagreement about what is, and what is not, justifiable disadvantage; there has been no shortage, over the years, of supporters of an hereditary principle.[200] The main opposition to this position stems, however, not from those who believe that disadvantage is just, but from those who do not accept that the redress of disadvantage is a legitimate concern. Nozick, for example, argues that a distribution of resources which stems from legitimate transactions must itself be legitimate, and that no attempt to redress the balance can be acceptable.[201] But this would be true only if no other principle permitted redistribution, and many principles do.

Redressing inequality is done by addressing the causes of disadvantage, but the nature of the response depends on the kind of inequality which is being addressed. Racial inequality is usually addressed by treating people alike, because racial differences are not generally relevant to the issues, like employment, housing and education, where disadvantage occurs most strongly. The response to gender inequalities, by contrast, has not been to treat men and women exactly alike, but to prevent differences between men and women being expressed in the structure of rewards and opportunities. Arguments for welfare have sought to protect and celebrate difference, rather than denigrating it.[202]

Redistribution

II.4.d   Social protection is redistributive.

Social protection is redistributive, in the sense that the services people receive are paid from a common pool, not from individual funds. People do not in general pay for a service at the point of delivery; they contribute to a scheme, and they draw on it when they are in need. Social services are also commonly redistributive over time – the point at which people pay for services is different from the point at which they will receive help. In a situation where all parties benefit (▸ I.3.b.i), it may not seem important whether the previous distributive balance is maintained. A concern with social justice, however, argues for a focus on redistributive outcomes.

Redistribution is conventionally classified as 'horizontal' or 'vertical'. Horizontal redistribution is redistribution from one category of people to another: from people of working age to old people, from people without

200 E.g. D. Hume (1888) *A treatise of human nature*, ed. L. Selby-Bigge, Oxford: Oxford University Press, pp. 501–513; Burke (1790).

201 R. Nozick (1974) *Anarchy, state and utopia*, Oxford: Blackwell.

202 F. Williams (1992) 'Somewhere over the rainbow: universality and diversity in social policy', in N. Manning and R. Page (eds) *Social policy review 4*, Canterbury: Social Policy Association.

children to people with children, from people who rent houses to those who buy them, and so forth. Vertical redistribution alters the distribution of income or wealth between rich and poor: progressive redistribution transfers resources from rich to poor, and regressive distribution transfers resources from poor to rich. Because social services and social protection are focused on need and conditions of dependency, they tend to be progressive in their intentions. There is however some debate as to whether they are progressive in effect.[203] Collective action, and in particular mutual aid, requires the ability to contribute, and that in turn implies a degree of economic stability. Where people are excluded, they are likely to be poor, or in precarious occupations. Solidarity tends, then, to redistribute horizontally; the development of vertical solidarity is far less firmly established, and more fragile.

II.4.d.i   Redistribution is intrinsic to solidarity.

The close identification of solidarity with mutual aid has led to solidarity being used at times as a synonym for redistribution.[204] There are other reasons besides solidarity why redistribution might take place – for example, as compensation for injury – and other forms of solidarity besides redistribution. The principle of solidarity is based on social obligations (▶ I.3.a), and there are forms of obligation which are not concerned with distributive issues. But solidarity is expressed through collective action, and collective action which is based in the obligations of solidarity leads to pooled resources, in the form of mutual aid and social organization (▶ II.3.a.ii). This, like other forms of social protection, is necessarily redistributive.

II.4.d.ii   The distribution of resources is a matter of convention.

The effect of interdependence in a developed economy is that production depends primarily on a process of exchange, rather than individual effort. People do not produce their own materials and tools in order to create things; they rely on the efforts of others (▶ I.1.a.i). Along with the myth of individualism (▶ I.1.b.ii), there is a recurring myth that individuals produce property. The identification of individualism with the defence of property has been one of the principal means by which a radical and subversive doctrine has come to act as a defence of the status quo. Property is produced through the division of labour in society.

---

203 J. Le Grand (1982) *The strategy of equality*, London: Allen and Unwin; R. Goodin and J. Le Grand (eds) (1987) *Not only the poor*, London: Allen and Unwin; J. Hills (ed.) (1996) *New inequalities*, Cambridge: Cambridge University Press.
204 E.g. J. Clasen (1997) 'Social insurance in Germany – dismantling or reconstruction?' in *Social insurance in Europe*, Bristol: Policy Press, pp. 63, 68.

The value of any good is determined by a range of factors; they include its utility, its scarcity, and possibly the labour which has been invested in it. Most of all, though, value is determined by the willingness and ability of people to pay; this is generally taken, in economics, as a sign of willingness to sacrifice other opportunities in order to gain the item. To a large extent, values reflect the conventional structure of resources and options. Value is, then, relative. Equally, that value is determined through society.

For the same reasons, the value of labour is conventional. There is no intrinsic rule which says that the value of a banker must be greater than that of a nursery worker, or that a sewage worker should be paid less than an estate agent; if anything, the scarcity of the skills, the responsibility of the post, and the importance of the function to society, suggests the opposite. But services to rich people generally command more than services to poor people, because the clients are better able to pay. There are other factors, of course, which are taken into consideration. Entry to some professions is controlled, in order to increase the price which the profession is able to command. Dirty work, like sewage treatment or refuse collection, is generally paid less than clean work. This seems to reflect social status, rather than the demands of the employment. Work predominantly undertaken by women is paid less than work predominantly undertaken by men. Where the gender balance in a profession shifts, as happened in secretarial and clerical work, the relative rewards of the profession tend to change with it.

This argument is fundamental to understanding the moral status of redistribution. The initial distribution stems from one set of social conventions, including the element of redistribution; redistribution itself derives from a related set of conventions.

II.4.d.iii   *Redistribution is part of the rules of the game.*

Redistribution is frequently represented in the literature as if it were some kind of distortion of the natural order: the conscious act of a meddlesome government in the delicate mechanisms of a society.[205] But much of the redistribution which takes place for the provision of social welfare is not like that: on the contrary, it stems from mutualist arrangements, freely entered into by the participants. Several countries, notably those in Northern Europe, have developed welfare systems without the element of compulsion (▶ I.3.b.iii(1)); others have welfare services substantially linked to mutualist associations, particularly trade unions. Redistribution is a normal aspect of social arrangements.

---

205 E.g. B. de Jouvenel (1951) *Ethics of redistribution*, Cambridge: Cambridge University Press; H. Acton (1971) *Morals of markets*, London: Longman; or Hayek, in P. Taylor-Gooby and J. Dale (1981) *Social theory and social welfare*, London: Arnold.

Another way of saying that something is a normal arrangement – not, that is, a commonplace arrangement, but one which is within the norms and expectations of a society – is that it is 'institutionalized' in society. A social institution is not necessarily a formal organization, but it is an established part of social life which is taken for granted as part of our social relationships and ordinary lives. Examples are the family, religious worship, or the use of money as a means of exchange. Redistribution is institutionalized, or built into the social fabric, in the same way. If redistribution is intrinsic to solidarity (▶ II.4.d.i), and solidarity is intrinsic to society (▶ I.3), then redistribution is intrinsic to society.

Redistribution between societies

II.4.e   There are related obligations to people in other countries.

Societies have obligations to other societies. First, there are the responsibilities which people in societies owe to social groups elsewhere, based in their relationships and contact with those people (▶ I.2.a.ii). Second, there are the obligations which societies owe to other societies (▶ I.4.e.iii). The general pattern of foreign aid is that it goes from one government to another (and not from a government to people in need in other countries).[206] The third responsibility is a basic humanitarian one, which is owed to every person; societies, too, are moral agents (▶ I.4.e.vi).

On all three counts, social responsibility cannot be considered to finish at the boundary of a society.

II.4.e.i   Justice, equality and redistribution are only applied in specific social contexts.

Although social responsibility can be extended across societies, there are important limitations in the concepts of justice, equality and redistribution which have been developed here. These concepts have to be applied in specific social contexts. People do not live in isolation, in an imaginary world where they have no relationships, obligations or rights; they begin as members of a society, with obligations structured in a specific social context. The groups and societies they are part of are not equal; some groups are disadvantaged relative to others. The effect of distributive justice within groups will not be the same as justice between groups. The same principle applies, evidently, between societies.

In theory, it should be possible to extend the principles of justice, equality and redistribution between societies. If a society is a meta-group, and there are responsibilities between societies, then there should

---

206 J. Eaton (1995) 'Foreign public capital flows', in J. Behrman and T. Srinivasan, *Handbook of development economics*, vol. 3B, Amsterdam: Elsevier.

be a case for redistribution between them. For redistribution between societies to have a major effect, though, obligations between societies would need to be considered before, or at least at the same time as, obligations within societies and social groups. But the structure of social obligations works in the opposite way: the obligations which are felt within groups are much stronger, and more keenly felt, than those which are felt between groups, and those which apply to societies as a whole are relatively weak. The strength of obligations diminishes with social distance (▶ I.3.a.i), and different groups are necessarily distant.

II.4.e.ii The scope of obligations to people in other countries is limited.

The needs of people in developing countries are serious: at the time of writing, the most important claims concern the inadequacies of water supplies, sanitation, drains, food and shelter.[207] However, the moral obligations I have identified do not address these issues very directly: the specific obligations of groups and societies to other societies do not seem to encompass them. In particular, the argument for direct redistribution is limited. Aid to developing countries tends to be characterized not so much by charitable donations as by concessionary terms: limited security for loans, reduced rates of interest, and extended loan periods. The scope of aid is limited, and the United Nations Development Program has commented that 'foreign aid has critical weaknesses – in quantity, equity, predictability and distribution'.[208] Aid is rarely based directly in humanitarian motives; it is commonly linked to economic and military activity, and to the interest of the donor country. The clearest case of this is 'tied aid', which imposes conditions that will benefit the donor, though there is an argument that all concern with economic development rather than meeting human needs is basically self-interested.[209] The proportion of income given in aid has been declining in recent years, and the UN emphasizes the importance of aid less and less. It has not completely given up on the idea, but most of its attention is devoted to other responses.

The responses which seem to be preferred reflect particular responsibilities, rather than generalized concern with humanitarianism or justice. There are two main examples. One is fair trade. Developed countries are being requested to stop weighting the game against the poorest countries. This includes, for example, the reduction of import

207 See e.g. M. Wuyts, M. Mackintosh and T. Hewitt (eds) (1992) *Development policy and public action*, Oxford: Oxford University Press; G. Rodgers (1995) *The poverty agenda and the ILO*, Geneva: ILO.

208 Cited in M. Todaro (1994) *Economic development*, New York: Longman, p. 526.

209 Eaton (1995).

restrictions and tariffs which make it difficult for developing countries to sell their produce.[210] The second is debt relief. Developing countries have extensive debts to the richer countries, and economically they are often crippled by interest payments. The issue of debt is covered by all three of the obligations to other countries, and the concern the issue has excited reflects its relative moral status.

This points to significant limitations in the moral framework which I have outlined. The emphasis on solidarity, reciprocity and interdependence helps to explain both the limited role played by development aid, and the restrictive conditions which are placed upon it. In a perfect world, obligations to strangers, or demands for justice across societies, should be at least equal to, and might even outweigh, the moral considerations which arise from the process of interaction and exchange. In terms of much of the theory developed here, and in practice, they do not.

---

210 United Nations Development Program (1997) *Human development report*, Oxford: Oxford University Press, ch. 4.

III THE STATE AND WELFARE

III The welfare state is a means of promoting and maintaining welfare in society.

III.1

THE ROLE OF THE STATE

III.1 'Government is a contrivance of human wisdom to provide for human wants.'

The nature of government
> III.1.a   *Government is a form of collective action.*
> III.1.a.i   Collective action by government is similar to other forms of collective action.
> III.1.a.ii States provide a framework for political action.

The state and society
> III.1.b   *The state is a part of society.*
> III.1.b.i   Government relates to a political community.
> III.1.b.ii Governments can act to maintain or change society.

Legitimate authority
> III.1.c   *Governments rely on authority.*
> III.1.c.i   The legitimacy of government derives from the morality of its actions.
> III.1.c.ii The purpose of government is to serve the interests of its citizens.

The nature of government

III.1.a   Government is a form of collective action.

Government is a set of formal structures, which are used to undertake a wide range of activities. Conventionally, the branches of government are distinguished as legislative (the formulation of rules), judicial (arbitration), and executive (the implementation of policy). More broadly, government tends to be identified with 'the state', a general term for the institutions and activities undertaken by governments. In so far as there is a distinction, states should be seen as institutions, rather than groups of people; they consist of a complex combination of agencies and procedures which together form the organizational means through which policy can be effected. Within states, 'governments' represent only the formal policy-making bodies. (This should not be taken to deny the potential of institutions within the state to generate their own rules and practices, which often acquire the status of policy.) These activities are all, necessarily, forms of collective action; they rely on concerted action within a received social framework.

III.1.a.i Collective action by government is similar to other forms of collective action.

In large part, the actions of states in the field of social welfare mirror the activity of other collective organizations. The actions are unusual mainly in their scope and coverage: most collective actions relate only to a limited part of society, but actions by the state often represent collective action at the level of the whole society.

There is a view, put by radical liberals, that the intervention of government relating to welfare is illegitimate.[211] Many of their objections assume that collective action by a government is based in coercion. That assumption is easy to dismiss: there have been governmental arrangements for social protection in several countries which have not been compulsory (▶ I.3.b.iii(2)). In the same light, it should not be supposed that compulsion is distinctively or uniquely the province of government: the arguments about free riders (▶ I.3.b.iii(1)) apply to other forms of collective action. Contracts of employment, to take the obvious example, do not reflect an individual negotiation between employer and employee, but more general terms of employment, often negotiated with a range of interested parties. A firm may reasonably decide to arrange social protection, like health or pensions, for its employees; it can do so economically and effectively through a comprehensive arrangement with a third party. In practice, this has meant for many that inclusion in collective arrangements is a condition of employment, and effectively compulsory – but that the element of compulsion is not attributable to government. In France, the national system of unemployment benefits is administered on the basis of an agreement between employers' and workers' organizations. Occupational pensions were initially introduced on a similar basis, though that scheme acquired a statutory basis in 1972.[212]

211 Nozick (1974); G. Brennan and D. Friedman (1981) 'A libertarian perspective on welfare', in P.G. Brown, C. Johnson and P. Vernier (eds) Income support: conceptual and policy issues, Totowa, NJ: Rowman and Littlefield.

212 J-C. Portonnier (1998) Les Termes français de la protection sociale, Paris: Mission-Recherche.

The functions associated with governance can and do exist outside the formal apparatus of a state. Employers can regulate activity; families can exercise control. Religious bodies form and arbitrate on rules; in many European societies, in parallel with the formal structures of government there are ecclesiastical, rabbinical and Islamic courts. Their authority depends on consent – and in the case of rabbinical courts, a ritual signifying consent to arbitration is a formal part of the process. Where such activities are generated through civil society, they are *prima facie* legitimate.

The forms of collective action which have been considered up to this point have been mainly non-governmental; they are developed and pursued beyond the scope of the state (▶ I.3.b.iv). In practice, the overlap between state action and other forms of collective action is considerable. In many countries, the process of providing welfare falls firmly within the province of such collective organizations, and it can be difficult to clarify the distinctions between such organizations and the formal apparatuses of the state. Collective action for welfare occurs because it is beneficial, desirable and part of human activity. It is unsurprising that governments should seek to engage in similar activity, and it seems perverse to argue that this kind of action is legitimate when it is undertaken by independent organizations, but illegitimate when it is undertaken by a government.

There are, however, two important objections which apply specifically to government action, as opposed to other forms of collective action. One, put by Hayek, is that even when government appears to be beneficent, there is a risk that the extension of its power and influence will corrupt the fabric of social life and lead to the abuse of its position.[213] There are some strong examples of this process taking place – Hayek was writing during the Nazi era. The point is not, however, sufficient to argue against government action. There are risks of abuse and damage in many actions which affect other people; the bigger the action, the greater the risk. Someone who sets up a business might put some competitors out of trade; there may be external costs imposed on other people; the time will come when employees have to be fired; many products carry risks for users. None of this is a reason not to set up in business; it is a reason to be wary about what one does, and to make sure that it is done properly, legitimately and considerately. The same reservations apply to governments: the power to change things for the better is also a power to make things worse – but it is not a reason for refusing to start.

The second objection is more difficult to discount, and more subtle; it was made, for example, by Herman Dooyeweerd in the Netherlands,[214]

---

213 F. Hayek (1944) *The road to serfdom*, London: Routledge and Kegan Paul.

214 P. Marshall (1985) 'Dooyeweerd's empirical theory of rights', in C.T. McIntire (ed.) *The legacy of Herman Dooyeweerd*, Lanham: University Press of America.

and it has been taken up in a different form by Michael Walzer.[215] Dooyeweerd argued that in any society there are distinct spheres of action: actions which are appropriate and legitimate in some social contexts may not be in others. 'Sphere sovereignty' argues for a separation of different areas of social life – for example, the separation of religion from government, the separation of commerce from education, or the separation of public and private spheres. We might argue (though the position depends on the society of which we are part) that the family is not an appropriate forum for the formal exercise of justice, that commercial relationships are not a good basis for sexual activity, or that the state has no role in emotional bonding. The boundaries of different spheres of influence shift, depending on the society where they are found, but the basic idea is an appealing one: legitimate action taken by one body can be illegitimate when it is taken by another outside the sphere.

This is a difficult argument to counter directly, because it depends largely on the mobilization of moral sentiments which differ according to social context. The separation of state and religion is evident to many people in the US and France; it is much less evident to many in England or Israel. In the Netherlands, welfare was traditionally organized around the 'pillars' of different religions; the organization of supportive social action was the province of the churches, not the state. For the argument to act as an objection to collective action for welfare there must be an identifiable sphere of influence, which leads to state action being distinct from other sorts of collective action, or defines collective action for welfare as the exclusive province of another aspect of social life. There may be a principle which makes it permissible for an employer, a trade union or a religious organization to arrange health care but debars government from doing so. Where there are such principles, however, they appear to be specific to particular cultures and political settlements.

This argument can be used to limit the scope of other forms of collective action, through families, businesses, associations or religious organizations. None of the objections considered – coercion, the balance of power or sphere sovereignty – clearly distinguishes the role of the state from that of other forms of collective action. Government is distinguished mainly by the strength of its powers, and its scope for action. This implies a heavy responsibility, as well as an opportunity for action; but the criteria by which collective actions have to be judged are essentially the same for government as they are for others.

III.1.a.ii States provide a framework for political action.

States are complex, diverse institutions which represent a range of interests, and within them governments are likely to pursue the interests

---

215 M. Walzer (1983) *Spheres of justice*, New York: Basic Books.

of a limited part of that range. The view of government as a form of collective action is ambiguous, because it is not always immediately clear what collectivity they represent. Societies are unequal, and within unequal structures people have different degrees of power (▶ I.2.c.i). The Marxist criticism of welfare as an exercise of power is based on the view that the actions of government are liable to serve the interests of the dominant class,[216] or at least of influential groups in a society.[217] I previously qualified this criticism by the suggestion that it would take a conscious exercise of power to alter the structure of disadvantage (▶ II.4.c.ii); and many governments have in fact intervened to moderate inequality, to deliver social protection and to pursue a modicum of social justice.[218] The view that government favours privileged groups is more true in developing countries, where government is likely to be seen, and to act, in a partisan role.[219] In most developed countries, the interplay of multiple actors makes it much more difficult to identify any consistent imbalance within the actions of government.[220]

The view this implies of government and the state is less one where governments are supreme bodies exercising ultimate control in a territory, and more one where they are policy actors engaged in negotiation with others. This position has been reinforced by changing patterns of social and economic relationships. Some of the factors driving change are supra-national in scope: the shift to 'global' (or sub-global) economic markets, the need to control multinational organizations and international crime, the effect of population movement, have encouraged governments to take a supra-national perspective. Other issues, like political pressures from increasingly articulate and skilled local populations, or the expanding range of state activities, have prompted localism and decentralization.[221] This has tended to imply a multi-tiered approach to governance. There has been, Jessop suggests, a 'hollowing-out' of the role of government: it may have the appearance of power, but the substance is less convincing, and such power as governments have has often been delegated, shifted downwards towards local initiatives, or upwards, to supra-national organizations.[222]

---

216 R. Miliband (1969) *The state in capitalist society*, London: Weidenfeld and Nicolson; H. Dean (1991) *Social security and social control*, London: Routledge.

217 C. Wright Mills (1956) *The power élite*, New York: Oxford University Press.

218 United Nations Development Program (1997).

219 The point is made by M. Lipton and M. Ravallion (1995) 'Poverty and policy', ch. 41 of Behrman and Srinivasan (1995) *Handbook of development economics*, vol. 3B, Amsterdam: Elsevier, pp. 2569–2570.

220 R. Dahl (1961) *Who governs?* New Haven, CT: Yale University Press.

221 United Nations Development Program (1997).

222 B. Jessop (1994) 'Post-Fordism and the state', in A. Amin (ed.) *Post Fordism: a reader*, Oxford: Blackwell.

This has led many states to search for new methods of working. Ironically, at the same time as new nation states are being formed in Europe in an effort to assert independent action – the division of Czechoslovakia, or the breakup of the former Soviet Union – other countries (and sometimes the same countries) have been seeking to join the European Union, which has a distinct federal structure. Federalism refers to a system of government in which citizens relate to governments at different levels;[223] in political terms, federal systems are commonly seen as a way of concealing local and national divisions, enabling co-operation by papering over the cracks.[224] One of the key characteristics of federalism is that it makes a citizen subject simultaneously to different regimes. This can limit the effective powers of government, but in some circumstances it can also widen the range of options for governmental action. The US War on Poverty was used by the federal government to expand its responsibilities for welfare;[225] a similar process has been undertaken by the European Union in the development of its social policy.[226]

The effect of the shift to multiple tiers of government may have been to reduce the impact of national governments, or at least their potential impact, on social and economic issues. But states retain two key roles: as the representatives of national interests, and as the legislative authority in particular locations. This guarantees them a major role as fora for political action – representing groups of people with a voice and a stake in the policy process – even if they do not necessarily determine outcomes in their own right.

The state and society

III.1.b   The state is a part of society.

The state functions in a social context: the system of laws, the rules of exchange and collective action are social and political at the same time. A system of government is not, in practice, distinct from social organization, and it is virtually impossible to distinguish social relationships from the relationships regulated by the state. I have referred to competing historical accounts, centred on one hand on the growth of solidarity, and on the other on the growing engagement of the state (▸ Method). Both are true, from different perspectives; they are not genuinely separable, because state and society have developed together.

---

223 K.C. Wheare (1946) *Federal government*, Oxford: Oxford University Press.

224 G. Smith (1995) 'Mapping the federal condition', in G. Smith (ed.) *Federalism: the multiethnic challenge*, London: Longman.

225 E. James (1970) *America against poverty*, London: Routledge, chs 7–8.

226 P. Spicker (1996) 'Social policy in a federal Europe', *Social Policy and Administration*, 30 (4): 293–304.

III.1.b.i   Government relates to a political community.

There is a degree of arbitrariness in the relationship of states to societies. One government may govern several different societies; one society may be fragmented between more than one state. Some states are remote from the societies they rule; others have been created artificially. States can be established, like the separation of Ireland from the UK, or extinguished, such as the incorporation of Hawaii into the United States, or Newfoundland into Canada. A state can be imposed on, or grafted on to, a society. Even if the reasons why states have been founded are good ones, it does not necessarily follow that their current status makes sense; lines of communication which were influential in the eighteenth or nineteenth centuries are not necessarily influential now. Some states govern very diverse, or divided populations; some are large coalitions of different social groups. There is no necessary link between the state and a nation or a culture.

The 'political community', though it may overlap with other kinds of community, is not directly equivalent to a society or social group; it is an artificial construct, referring to people who are subject to a particular political and legal regime, and who have rights in relation to it. Although there are important differences between the political community and the society, there is inevitably an overlap between the two. The development of political communities invariably fosters interaction and interdependence; it implies cultural diffusion, or the exportation of values, and there are many cases where shared political institutions have led to the imposition of common practices on different cultures. Even if government and society are distinct, they are intimately connected, and it can be difficult to know where one ends and the other begins.

III.1.b.ii   Governments can act to maintain or change society.

Although government is part of society, a government can also try to change a society; governments and states are agents of maintenance and change. Governments maintain society because stability and cohesion are part of the things which people want them to achieve; this is the justification for the attempt of modern governments to stabilize the economy.[227] Governments change society in so far as they alter what would otherwise have been true. Maintenance and change are two sides of the same coin: patterns of social behaviour and relationships are in a constant state of flux, and both maintenance and change involve an understanding of the dynamics of change. The direction of changes in society can be seen as a form of 'social policy', but the term 'social policy' is usually used much more modestly to refer to the development of

---

227 S.J. Bailey (1995) *Public sector economics*, Basingstoke: Macmillan, ch. 2.

social welfare services; for that reason, Ferge proposed the use of the term 'societal' or 'structural' policy to distinguish the kinds of policy intended to maintain or change social relationships.[228]

Whether or not changes are happening depends, in large part, on how one defines a change. The more pluralistic and complex a society appears, the more difficult it is to see any change as making a significant difference to the overall pattern of social relationships in its own right. It is true that certain social developments have rippled through different aspects of society, changing many different sectors at the same time. Examples include the aftermath of the second world war, the revolution in communications, the development of mass culture, and the growth of global systems of exchange. Family life, neighbourhoods, economic markets and nationality have been profoundly affected by each of these changes. At the same time, it is striking how little these changes have seemed to be in the control of governments, and the belief that a government has the power fundamentally to alter a society is difficult to sustain.

Legitimate authority

III.1.c   Governments rely on authority.

Government and the state are distinguished from other forms of association mainly by the primacy of their authority over other agencies. Authority is a moral term; it consists of the right to undertake actions, or to constrain the actions of others. Max Weber described the state as having 'the monopoly of the legitimate use of physical force within a given territory'.[229] This is not universally true; the foundation of the United States was based on the principle that people needed to be able to defend themselves against tyrannical force, and consequently the authority to use force is shared in the constitution between the government and the citizenry. The same kind of reservation restricts the scope of government in the US in relation to other spheres of social life, including the press and religious worship.

The authority exercised by government means that others will defer to it – another case, socially, of something being true because people accept it as true. Authority makes it possible to govern – to establish a framework of rules, and so to establish the conditions under which other associations work. It also makes it possible to coerce people, and that is fundamental to achieving some of the outcomes which states achieve;

---

228 Z. Ferge (1979) *A society in the making*, Harmondsworth: Penguin, p. 55.
229 Weber, in H. Gerth and C. Wright Mills (eds) (1991) *From Max Weber*, London: Routledge, p. 78.

powers of coercion lie behind the imposition of minimum standards which are basic to welfare provision.

The primacy of government is sanctioned because the exercise of authority is seen as legitimate. States acquire legitimacy in a variety of ways, particularly through election, because that seems to represent the stated wishes of the citizenry. However, many states are considered legitimate just because they are there; it may be difficult to justify the existence of undemocratic countries which result from the partition of previous countries, like Kuwait or the Yugoslavian Republic. Some governments, particularly in Europe, have emerged historically as a result of the concentration of physical force, but that does not justify the assumption (made, for example, by Nozick)[230] that the main purpose of the early state is physical protection. Many states are creations of the twentieth century; they have developed because of the breakup of ancient empires, and the movement from colonialism. Even when they have resulted from settlements following wars, the motive forces have been arguments for national self-determination and the need for governance. Recently, there has been a proliferation of new governments, representing new, or re-emergent, nations; examples are Slovenia, Estonia and Slovakia. They are being developed, not only to provide defence, but to do the kinds of things which governments do: to administer the society, to develop the economy, to deliver social welfare, and to offer a political forum where people's wishes can be heard. The position of the state can be seen as a practical necessity: these are important tasks, and the acceptance of the authority of the state as legitimate is essential to the performance of these functions.

III.1.c.i   *The legitimacy of government derives from the morality of its actions.*

The legitimacy of a government is a description of its moral status; a legitimate government is one which is morally accepted. There are two conditions which must be satisfied for a government to be morally accepted. First, it must have proper authority for its actions, which indicates moral acceptance of its accession and continuation in power. A government which is not legitimately instituted cannot take legitimate action in effect, because it has no authority to tax, to spend, to regulate or to coerce beyond the rights of ordinary citizens. Second, the actions of the government must themselves be legitimate, which requires conformity to accepted rules.

Many philosophers have sought to derive the legitimacy of government from its foundation: the authority of government has been attributed, for example, to the dispositions of a benign divinity, to its historical

---

230 Nozick (1974).

relationship with the people or to popular consent.[231] Some governments which have acceded to power legitimately have acted in an illegitimate way; the supreme example is the rise to power of Adolf Hitler, who became Chancellor of Germany through a legitimate process of election. Conversely, governments can be legitimate even if the foundation of the system was not. The basis for the constitutional monarchy of the United Kingdom is questionable, and its parliamentary system is deeply flawed, but over time it has gained a high degree of moral acceptance, and few people would deny that the system is, more or less, legitimate.

Legitimate accession is important for legitimacy, but it is not sufficient. An action which is immoral is immoral irrespective of who does it, and actions which are not morally acceptable cannot be legitimate. The proper test of legitimate government is, then, whether it acts legitimately.

III.1.c.ii   *The purpose of government is to serve the interests of its citizens.*

The quotation which heads this chapter comes from Edmund Burke.[232] It describes, perhaps, the way things ought to be rather than the way that they are, but it is also a key statement of the foundation and purposes of government. Government is a form of collective action, but it is a form which in certain circumstances may claim primacy over other forms of action. In some cases, the actions of government will be partisan, or confined to the interests of a limited number of people; but the central justification for the primacy of government is that it represents the interests of the people who are subject to it, rather than the interests of specific groups or factions within it.

The authority exercised by contemporary governments is intimately bound up with the concept of citizenship. The idea of citizenship was referred to previously in the context of social rights, where it has a range of meanings, both legal and social (▶ II.2.c.iv). In the political sense, a citizen is a member of a political community, holding rights in relation to government, state and society. Political citizenship is different from membership of a society; people can be political citizens even if they are socially excluded, and conversely they can be members of a society without having the rights of political citizens. The importance of the concept in the literature of social policy is indicative of a strong identification of welfare with political status rather than its social base.[233]

---

231 See E. Barker (ed.) (1971) *Social contract: essays by Locke, Hume and Rousseau,* Oxford: Oxford University Press.

232 E. Burke (1790) *Reflections on the revolution in France,* New York: Holt, Rinehart and Winston.

233 E.g. J. Parker (1975) *Social policy and citizenship,* London: Macmillan; D. Heater (1990) *Citizenship,* Harlow: Longman; G. Andrews (ed.) (1991) *Citizenship,* London: Lawrence and Wishart.

Political citizenship gives the citizen both a status as someone holding rights, and a means of holding government to account. The development of political rights has been a major element in the history of the welfare states, constraining and guiding governments towards a greater commitment to social protection.[234]

Accountability has been central to this process. Governments are not simply beneficial organizations, and it would be naive to suppose that a commitment to public service could be adequate to explain the direction of public policy. Governments are subject, though, to many pressures, and for many governments these pressures include a concern with electoral advantage. This means that governments are likely to be sensitive to the expression of the wishes (or demands) of their citizens.[235] In these circumstances, many governments have come to pursue, however imperfectly, the interests of their citizens.

234 T.H. Marshall (1981) *The right to welfare*, London: Heinemann.
235 J. Schumpeter (1967) 'Two concepts of democracy', in A. Quinton (ed.) *Political philosophy*, Oxford: Oxford University Press.

III.2

THE WELFARE STATES

III.2 The welfare states provide social protection.

The state and welfare

III.2.a	*Legitimate governments protect the welfare of their citizens.*
III.2.a.i	Salus populi suprema est lex.
III.2.a.ii	Democratic governments secure welfare.

Securing welfare

III.2.b	*Governments have to secure the preconditions for welfare.*
III.2.b.i	Governments have to foster economic development.
III.2.b.ii	Governments have to protect the rights of their citizens.
III.2.b.iii	Governments have to promote social cohesion and basic security.

The provision of welfare

III.2.c	*Someone has to provide social protection.*
III.2.c.i	It doesn't have to be done by government.
III.2.c.ii	In the last resort, government has the duty by default.
III.2.c.iii	The provider of last resort has to offer more than the last resort.
III.2.c.iv	The provision of welfare commits governments to redistribution.

The welfare states

III.2.d	*The welfare states are simply institutional forms of social protection.*
III.2.d.i	Social protection exists without the state.
III.2.d.ii	There is more than one kind of welfare state.
III.2.d.iii	The welfare states elude classification.

The state and welfare

III.2.a Legitimate governments protect the welfare of their citizens.

If governments serve the interests of their citizens, they will do the kinds of things which the citizens want them to do, or from which they believe the citizens will benefit.[236] These activities will often include action related to social protection. Social protection is necessary for welfare (► II.3), it requires collective action (► II.3.a.i), and it is not sufficiently provided through the market (► II.3.b). In consequence, it is something which an economically rational, self-interested group of citizens will probably want. (This may imply that the government develops a system of social protection, but the question of whether a government should provide social protection itself is distinct, and will be returned to later.)

The corollary of this position is that governments which wish to be seen as legitimate may pursue welfare policy in order to demonstrate it. Neo-Marxists have described welfare provision, dismissively, as a form of 'legitimation', an attempt to make an unpalatable political process acceptable to the mass of people.[237] If the purpose of government is to serve the interest of its citizens, a government which acts to secure social protection is more legitimate than one that does not.

III.2.a.i Salus populi suprema est lex.

One of the most ancient precepts of political science is the argument that governments exist to promote welfare: 'the welfare of the people is the highest law'.[238] That principle is consistent with the argument that government has an instrumental purpose, but it goes beyond it. The legitimacy of a government depends, in large part, on whether it seeks to promote the welfare of its people.

There is a problem with this formulation, which is that a government might seek to promote welfare through illegitimate means: for example, by making war against a neighbouring state. The rearmament of Germany in the 1930s undoubtedly helped to revitalize the economy and to combat unemployment. The impact of colonial expeditions in the nineteenth century was primarily to enrich the colonial nations at the expense of their colonies. A concern for welfare is necessary for legitimacy, but it is not sufficient for it.

---

236 Both definitions of interest are in B. Barry (1965) *Political argument*, London: Routledge and Kegan Paul, pp. 187–188.

237 J. Habermas (1984) 'What does a legitimation crisis mean today? Legitimation problems in late capitalism', in W. Connolly (ed.) *Legitimacy and the state*, Oxford: Blackwell; C. Offe (1984) *Contradictions of the welfare state*, London: Hutchinson.

238 T. Hobbes (1651) *Leviathan*, Harmondsworth: Penguin, 1968.

III.2.a.ii Democratic governments secure welfare.

Democracy has been defined as government of the people, by the people and for the people. It is characterized partly by the process of electing a government, but so many elections are unfree – confined to one party, or one set of approved candidates – that this is hardly enough to define the process. Much more important is the identification of democracy with liberal values – the rights of individual citizens to obtain redress against governments, or against each other.

Governments which are described as democratic are not uniquely concerned with welfare. In the course of the twentieth century, welfare systems, with extensive rationales, were developed in Fascist and communist governments. What these systems had in common was the deliberate exclusion of certain parties from the remit of social protection. Fascist social policy was characterized by the dominance of the nation, a strong emphasis on socialization into the moral dominance of the collectivity, an idealized family policy and eugenics intended to lead to a 'desirable' pattern of births.[239] Communist social policy combined the central role of labour with the exclusion and social rejection of parasites.[240] Non-democratic governments may also secure welfare, but they do not do it for everyone. Democracy, by contrast, implies universalist concerns.

Democratic government is so widely practised, and so widely abused, that it is difficult to identify the ideal with the reality. The rights of the poorest citizens in democratic countries seem so fragile that they hardly seem to offer real protection. In the US, single parents who objected to midnight searches by benefits agencies were told that they did of course have a constitutional right, but if they chose to exercise it they must expect their benefits to be stopped.[241] In the UK, a homeless family which went to court to protest at being placed in accommodation that was unfit for human habitation was told that it was still accommodation, and that they had no protection.[242]

And yet, the strongest argument for democracy is made by Drèze and Sen, in their work on famines: there has never been a famine in a

---

239 R. Grunberger (1974) *A social history of the Third Reich*, Harmondsworth: Penguin; G. Rimlinger (1987) 'Social policy under German fascism', in M. Rein, G. Esping-Anderson and L. Rainwater (eds) *Stagnation and renewal in social policy*, New York: Sharpe; P. Weindling (1989) *Health, race and German politics between national unification and Nazism, 1870–1945*, Cambridge: Cambridge University Press.

240 V. George and N. Manning (1980) *Socialism, social welfare and the Soviet Union*, London: Routledge and Kegan Paul; R. Beerman (1959 *et seq.*) 'The law against parasites, tramps and beggars', *Soviet Studies*, 9 (2), 11 (4), 13 (2).

241 F. Piven and R. Cloward (1971) *Regulating the poor*, London: Tavistock.

242 R. v *London Borough of Hillingdon, ex parte* Pulhofer, 1986 All ER 734; 18 HLR 158, HL.

democracy. Drèze and Sen argue that it reflects the more widespread dispersion of entitlements in a democracy; where people have no rights, they are not able to make use of the resources that exist.[243] But it is difficult to show here just what the causal link is, or if there is one; it may be true that adherence to democracy has no more basis than the superstition which sends football players to important matches tying their shoelaces in the same order as they did for their last big game. Possibly it reflects the political power of the electorate; possibly it shows the respect which democracy generates for the citizen; and possibly democracy itself depends on the material conditions which lead to the avoidance of famine.

Securing welfare

III.2.b   Governments have to secure the preconditions for welfare.

If governments have to secure welfare, and there are preconditions for welfare to be achieved, governments have to secure those preconditions. The preconditions which were identified earlier had three main elements: economic development, social cohesion and security, and a structure of rights (▶ II.2).

Securing preconditions is not necessarily equivalent to meeting conditions directly; the conditions may be met in other ways, through existing social arrangements. The responsibility of government does imply, though, a responsibility to monitor circumstances, and to intervene as appropriate to ensure that the conditions are met. The idea that governments 'have' to do this is ambiguous. Part of the obligation is moral; rights exist because there are moral obligations which validate the claims. Part is political. One implication of accountability to an electorate is that a government that fails to undertake these functions adequately is liable to lose power.

III.2.b.i   Governments have to foster economic development.

The responsibility of governments to foster economic development is very much of this type. There are strongly opposing schools of thought among economists: some 'neo-classicists' hold that most of the mechanisms of the economy are self-regulating if left to their own devices, while others argue (after Keynes) that many economic systems are unstable, and intervention

---

243 J. Drèze and A. Sen (1989) *Hunger and public action*, Oxford: Clarendon Press.

and management are essential to development. Historically, the development of the modern welfare states was strongly linked with the latter point of view.[244] In the post-war period, the provision of welfare was seen as an economic regulator, directly complementing the management of the economy.[245] The 'New Right' rejected that view, arguing that public expenditure represented a threat to economic stability;[246] and Marxist critics seized on the same arguments to claim that this position revealed fundamental contradictions in the nature of the welfare state.[247]

There is no evidence to support this position. In general, it is true that countries which are more developed are also more likely to have developed welfare systems, but this does not show that one factor causes another. Reviewing evidence from a number of developed countries, Atkinson found that there are as many examples of states which combine economic growth and expenditure on welfare as there are of those whose expenditure is linked with poor economic performance.[248]

III.2.b.ii   *Governments have to protect the rights of their citizens.*

Government regulates the conduct of relationships between citizens. The primary redress of the weak against the strong is the rule of law, which guarantees people's rights against exploitation and abuse. The clearest example is criminal law, which protects persons and property. This restricts the behaviour of some in order to protect the rights of all. There are many more rights, however, than the rights of the person and property (▶ II.2). Social and economic rights have been a fundamental part of the development of relationships in the nineteenth and twentieth centuries, and liberal democratic governments have accordingly acted in order to protect them.

The expansion of rights is liable to abuse by governments. There are problems of patronage and 'clientelism' (which Americans call the 'pork barrel') in Southern European countries, where politicians reward political favour through welfare systems.[249] Dicey, the legal theorist, saw

---

244 V. George and P. Wilding (1994) *Welfare and ideology*, Hemel Hempstead: Prentice-Hall.

245 E.g. J.H. Richardson (1960) *Economic and financial aspects of social security*, London: Allen and Unwin.

246 D.S. King (1987) *The new right*, London: Macmillan.

247 See R. Klein (1993) 'O'Goffe's tale', in C. Jones (ed.) *New perspectives on the welfare state in Europe*, London: Routledge.

248 A.B. Atkinson (1995) *Incomes and the welfare state*, Cambridge: Cambridge University Press, ch. 6.

249 C. Saraceno and N. Negri (1994) 'The changing Italian welfare state', *Journal of European Social Policy*, 4 (1): 19–34; M. Ferrera (1996) 'The "Southern Model" of welfare in social Europe', *Journal of European Social Policy*, 6 (1): 17–37.

the constant push to deliver personal benefits as a major part of the impetus to collectivism.[250] But the converse may also be true; the response to electoral pressure may lead governments to reduce the rights of people in need where a sizeable bloc of voters are opposed to provision. Some governments have abolished existing rights, and during the 1980s there was widespread retrenchment in rights-based benefits.[251] This has included universal systems, like pensions in New Zealand, and even rights which people have paid for: since the early 1980s British governments have replaced a range of insurance-based benefits with more restricted alternatives, including benefits for unemployment, sickness and maternity.

III.2.b.iii   Governments have to promote social cohesion and basic security.

The responses of governments to issues of social cohesion and security are mixed. It is not always clear what kind of policy will support social cohesion; it is not even certain that social cohesion is desirable, because so much depends on the form that it takes. It is not difficult to find agreement that some extremes are undesirable: civil war or racial strife are best avoided, while disappearances and torture are not consistent with basic security. Beyond this, there is no clear consensus. Because individualism is strong in liberal democracies, measures which focus on social relationships – such as family policy or community development – may not feature prominently on the political agenda. At the same time, many governments are committed to the extension of solidarity, which has become a major theme in the social policy of the European Union.

The substantive issue on which there seems to be broadest agreement is social protection, but the conditions under which governments are willing to engage in social protection are complex, and this requires further development in the sections which follow.

The provision of welfare

III.2.c   Someone has to provide social protection.

Social protection is basic to the maintenance of welfare, and people are not necessarily able to provide it for themselves. I have argued that social protection, because it is a way of guaranteeing people's positions, can only be provided for through collective action (▶ II.3.a.i). Social

---

250 A.V. Dicey (1914) *Lectures on the relation between law and public opinion in England during the nineteenth century*, London: Macmillan, 1948.

251 H. Glennerster and J. Midgley (eds) (1991) *The radical right and the welfare state*, Hemel Hempstead: Harvester Wheatsheaf.

protection does happen spontaneously, but it does not happen for everyone, and it does not necessarily cover all the needs people would wish it to cover. If social protection is to be provided for those who are excluded, someone has to take it on.

Social protection is generally thought to be desirable, and governments have often attempted to provide it. If government is intended to provide for human wants, and people want social protection, governments will do it. This much is unsurprising, and unexceptional.

Beyond this, it can be argued that there is a moral obligation to provide social protection. This has three main elements, all of which have been discussed in previous sections. First, there are general obligations of solidarity to others in society. People have duties to others in society (▶ I.3.a), and people in need have correlative rights. Second, there are mutual obligations based on generalized reciprocity (▶ I.1.c.i). Once the process of obligation has begun, relationships are set in motion which generate obligations in other people. Everyone who receives benefits from the previous generation acquires responsibilities, not only to them, but to other generations (▶ I.1.c.ii(3)). Third, there is a responsibility on government to promote the welfare of the people (▶ III.2.a.i).

III.2.c.i   It doesn't have to be done by government.

There is nothing within this system of obligations which says that government must provide welfare itself. Governments have a wide range of options to ensure that social protection is provided, and it may well be that protection is adequately provided through existing arrangements. There have been many cases where aspects of social protection have been substantially delivered through non-governmental forms of collective action: examples can be drawn from Sweden,[252] Denmark,[253] or France.[254] Unemployed people in France are principally dealt with through an agreement of employers and trade unions, and employers and employees both contribute to benefits. (The government subsequently commissioned this independent service to provide an additional benefit, the *allocation de solidarité spécifique,* for those whose entitlements to benefits are exhausted. It is the ASS, rather than the contributory

---

252 A. Gould (1996) 'Sweden: the last bastion of social democracy', in V. George and P. Taylor-Gooby (eds) *European welfare policy: squaring the welfare circle,* London: Macmillan.

253 J. Kvist (1997) 'Retrenchment or restructuring? The emergence of a multitiered welfare state in Denmark', in J. Clasen (ed.) *Social insurance in Europe,* Bristol: Policy Press.

254 M-T. Join-Lambert, A. Bolot-Giottler, C. Daniel, D. Lenoir and D. Méda (1994) *Politiques sociales,* Paris: Presses de la Fondation Nationale des Sciences Politiques/Dalloz.

system, which has been the focus of recent social protests by unemployed people.)[255]

This is not the kind of arrangement which has been made through 'privatization'.[256] Privatization has been motivated by a desire to inject the values of the marketplace into the provision of welfare. It encompasses not only the transfer of resources between sectors, but movement from traditional providers to large corporate providers,[257] the purchase of services from the private sector[258] and the conversion of state services to market principles.[259] Privatization has been a highly ideological movement, and its advocates have not always distinguished between the operation of state and autonomous producers whose activities have been undertaken on a collectivist or mutualist basis. In the UK, it has led to withdrawal of state involvement from the voluntary sector in housing,[260] and the conversion to the market of mutualist financial institutions and building societies. The health care system in Israel was founded on a mutualist basis by the trade unions movement, and at its peak it covered nearly 90 per cent of the population. The Israeli government took the view that this system suffered from the vices of monopolistic provision, and subsequently arranged for the breakup of the health service into distinct, competing units.[261]

The argument for privatization rests on a belief in the superiority of market provision over collective action. The central problem with this approach is that, although commercial markets can often offer effective provision of aspects of social services, the overall protection they offer is deficient (▸ II.3.b), and states necessarily continue to have residual responsibilities.

255 A. Chemin and C. Monnot (1998) 'Lionel Jospin n'apaise pas la colère des mouvements de chômeurs', Le Monde, 23 January.

256 J. Legrand and R. Robinson (1984) Privatisation and the welfare state, London: Macmillan; N. Johnson (1989) 'The privatization of welfare', Social Policy and Administration, 23 (1): 17–30. The most influential example is described in S. Borutzy (1991) 'The Chicago Boys, social security and welfare in Chile', in H. Glennerster and J. Midgley (eds) The radical right and the welfare state, Hemel Hempstead: Harvester Wheatsheaf.

257 D. Stoesz and H. Karger (1991) 'The corporatisation of the US welfare state', Journal of Social Policy, 20 (2): 157–172.

258 S. Shaw (1990) 'Privatising prison services', in R. Parry (ed.) Privatisation, London: Jessica Kingsley.

259 E. Granaglia (1997) 'The Italian National Health Service and the challenge of privatization', in B. Palier (ed.) Comparing social welfare systems in Southern Europe, vol. 3, Paris: MIRE.

260 B. Randolph (1993) 'The reprivatisation of housing associations', in P. Malpass and R. Means (eds) Implementing housing policy, Buckingham: Open University Press.

261 Y. Zalmanovitch (1997) 'Some antecedents to healthcare reform: Israel and the US', Policy and Politics, 25 (3): 251–268.

III.2.c.ii   *In the last resort, government has the duty by default.*

The central problem for government is that it becomes, by default, the provider of last resort; coverage of the excluded is done by government, or it is not done at all. (People are excluded because they are not covered by other means. This is virtually tautologous, which is why more extensive discussion is not really necessary.)

What happens if provision is not made for people who are excluded? The answer may, genuinely, be nothing; certainly, several developed countries, including Germany and Italy, have managed successful economies over time with very little effective coverage for their excluded groups.[262] This is possible, partly, because there may be other mechanisms of support, including families, voluntary organizations and charities; and partly because countries and systems can continue to function if the numbers of people who suffer are relatively few. But it happens at a cost. Some of the cost is felt by those who are excluded. Germany, prior to unification, excluded a small minority of unemployed people,[263] but it had almost full employment; subsequent to unification, the system now offers little protection for large numbers of people.[264] Italy has problems of exclusion, homelessness and begging,[265] which only recently have led to moves to develop a national programme for social integration.[266] Some of the cost is felt because people are not covered, and suffer insecurity as a result. Other consequences may still be experienced by those who are covered by their own arrangements, like the problems of disease, street begging, and the fear of crime. Whether this is considered tolerable depends on the numbers and influence of the people affected,

---

262 M. Wilson (1993) 'The German welfare state: a conservative regime in crisis', in A. Cochrane and J. Clarke (eds) *Comparing welfare states*, London: Sage; J. Clasen and R. Freeman (ed.) (1994) *Social policy in Germany*, Hemel Hempstead: Harvester Wheatsheaf; M. Ferrera (1986) 'Italy', in P. Flora (ed.) *Growth to limits*, Berlin: de Gruyter; U. Ascoli (1988) 'The Italian welfare system in the 1980s', in R. Morris (ed.) *Testing the limits of social welfare*, Hanover, NH: Brandeis University Press.

263 R. Mitton, P. Wilmott and P. Wilmott (1983) *Unemployment, poverty and social policy in Europe*, London: Bedford Square Press.

264 H. Ganssman (1993) 'After unification', *Journal of European Social Policy*, 3 (2): 79–90; Wilson (1993) 'The German welfare state: a conservative regime in crisis', in A. Cochrane and J. Clarke (eds) *Comparing welfare states*, London: Sage.

265 E. Reyneri (1994) 'Italy: a long wait in the shelter of the family and of safeguards from the state', in O. Benoit-Guilbot and D. Gallie (eds) *Long term unemployment*, London: Pinter; E. Morlicchio (1996) 'Exclusion from work and the impoverishment processes in Naples', in E. Mingione (ed.) *Urban poverty and the underclass*, Oxford: Blackwell; A. Mitchison (1987) 'Down and out in Naples', *New Society*, 20 February: 16–18.

266 MISEP (European Commission Employment Observatory) (1998) *Policies no. 64*, Winter: 23–24.

and the political construction put on the problems. If government tries to avoid negative consequences for society, and tries to do what people want, it is likely to do something for excluded people; and it does it, in the last resort, because no one else does.

III.2.c.iii   The provider of last resort has to offer more than the last resort.

Some governments have sought to provide welfare on a residual basis, as the safety net for circumstances when everything else has failed. In principle, this has much to commend it: it implies a tightly focused, efficient service, minimal interference in the economy, and effective redistribution to those in need. In practice, however, the general experience has been that it doesn't work. The first problem is that the boundaries are unclear; focusing provision only on those in the greatest need is administratively cumbersome and inefficient, and liable not to reach those to whom it is directed.[267] Second, residual welfare produces perverse effects, favouring those who have not made provision for themselves over those who have.[268] Third, residual welfare is bitterly resented, by donors as well as by recipients; it creates a sense of welfare as a 'public burden', and leads to a division between the dependent poor and others.[269] Finally, though it is not a fundamental objection, residual provision is expensive: targeting those whose needs are greater, and who cannot be dealt with profitably by the private sector means necessarily that they will cost more than others to provide for.

The general experience of governments working in this field is that the boundaries of residual welfare cannot be maintained. The history of the English Poor Law was one of inexorable, progressive expansion, despite the resistance of administrators. There were persistent problems of equity, because people who were only marginally better off than recipients did not receive benefits. It was impossible in practice to make the condition of paupers 'less eligible', or less to be chosen, than that of independent labourers:[270] paupers were fed, educated and received medical care, and the workhouses in some areas were described as

---

267 A. Deacon and J. Bradshaw (1983) *Reserved for the poor*, Oxford: Blackwell; J. Bradshaw (1985) 'Tried and found wanting', in S. Ward (ed.) *DHSS in crisis: social security – under pressure and review*, London: CPAG; A.B. Atkinson (1991) *The social safety net*, London: LSE Welfare State Programme; G. Cornia and F. Stewart (1995) 'Food subsidies: two errors of targeting', in F. Stewart, *Adjustment and poverty*, London: Routledge.

268 F. Field (1996) *Stakeholder welfare*, London: IEA Health and Welfare Unit.

269 R.M. Titmuss (1974) *Social Policy: an introduction*, London: Allen and Unwin.

270 S.G. Checkland and E. Checkland (eds) (1974) *The Poor Law Report of 1834*, Harmondsworth: Penguin.

'pauper palaces'.[271] This is inconsistent with social justice, and there were recurring pressures either to reduce the quality of provision for paupers – which led to notable scandals[272] – or to extend these facilities to others, which ultimately is what happened. The driving force behind the expansion, though, was that the conditions of sickness and unemployment which the Poor Law was dealing with were endemic, and beyond the control of the recipients.

Part of the experience of the Poor Law, too, was that a failure to deal with one set of problems led to displacement: problems were presented to the authorities in a different form. Edwin Chadwick's *Report on the sanitary condition of the labouring population of Great Britain* was prompted by the realization that dependency on the Poor Law reflected the needs of sick people, and the levels of sickness reflected the lack of public health provision.[273] In the absence of one kind of provision, people in need had to be diverted towards another. This became part of the received wisdom of the administration: the same logic prevailed in the Beveridge Report, which 'assumed' health services and policies for full employment as necessary conditions for the successful operation of social insurance.[274]

III.2.c.iv   *The provision of welfare commits governments to redistribution.*

Governments may be committed to redistribution as a matter of principle: if there is a general social objective of social justice, however it is understood, then governments are responsible for it. Redistribution is intrinsic to the maintenance of social protection (▸ II.4.d), and governments, once they have become responsible for the provision of welfare, must inevitably be concerned with distributive issues. In so far as they are providing welfare themselves, they are altering the distribution of resources, and by their actions they come to bear a responsibility for the distributive consequences.

There are two principles here – social justice, and social protection – and potentially they may conflict. In both cases there is an initial presumption in favour of equality, because fair dealing implies equality unless there are reasons to the contrary (▸ II.4.c.iii). However, the general objective of social justice implies a concern with distributive outcomes overall. By contrast, the requirement to deal fairly with people usually refers specifically to the sphere of activity in which the government is

---

271 A. Digby (1978) *Pauper palaces*, London: Routledge and Kegan Paul.

272 I. Anstruther (1973) *The scandal of the Andover workhouse*, London: Geoffrey Bles.

273 S.E. Finer (1952) *The life and times of Sir Edwin Chadwick*, London: Methuen.

274 W. Beveridge (1942) *Social insurance and allied services* Cmd 6404, London: HMSO.

engaged. (An example is the distribution of health care provision.)[275] Social justice cannot be achieved just by ensuring that social services act equitably, because an equitable approach in one sphere which fails to address inequities elsewhere may produce inequitable results overall. It may even reinforce those inequities (▶ II.4.a.i).

The welfare states

III.2.d The welfare states are simply institutional forms of social protection.

The 'welfare states' of developed countries were based, in most cases, on the existing patterns of social protection which had been generated through collective social action. The Bismarckian scheme of social insurance, the model for Germany and much of continental Europe, drew directly on the experience of workers' organizations in order to provide a model of stable finance and membership.[276] In several countries, the state complemented or supplemented the provision made by mutual aid organizations.[277] In others, notably the United Kingdom, it took them over: despite the Beveridge Report's concern to protect the scope of action of the Friendly Societies,[278] the desire for a uniform national scheme led to the obliteration of differences. But the Beveridge scheme was still represented, at the time of its introduction, as a form of mutual insurance, and of national solidarity:

> The scheme as a whole will embrace, not certain occupation and income groups, but the entire population. Concrete expression is thus given to the solidarity and unity of the nation, which in war have been its bulwarks against aggression and in peace will be its guarantees of success in the fight against individual want and mischance.[279]

The Beveridge Report became a symbol of the kind of society the Allies were fighting for – it was dropped by parachute into occupied territory[280] – and it was profoundly influential in the reconstruction of post-

---

275 C. Propper and R. Upward (1991) *Need, equity and the NHS: the distribution of health care expenditure 1974–1987*, Bristol: School for Advanced Urban Studies; and see J. Pereira (1993) 'What does equity in health mean?', *Journal of Social Policy*, 22 (1): 19–48.

276 W.J. Mommsen (1981) *The emergence of the welfare state in Britain and Germany*, Beckenham: Croom Helm.

277 P. Baldwin (1990) *The politics of social solidarity*, Cambridge: Cambridge University Press.

278 Beveridge (1942).

279 Cmd 6550, 1944, *Social insurance*, London: HMSO, p. 6.

280 J-J. Dupeyroux (1989) *Droit de la sécurité sociale*, Paris: Dalloz, p. 72n.

war Europe. The post-war welfare states represented the extension of state activity into a field previously dominated by the mechanisms of collective action: the formal institution of social protection as a social responsibility.

III.2.d.i Social protection exists without the state.

The welfare states came late to the principle of social protection, and many have been based on developed systems run by existing institutions. Often these have been linked to the industrial process; the formal basis of welfare provision commonly rests on institutions founded and paid for by employers, employees or some combination of the two.[281] Their foundation, and their legitimacy, rests in the legitimacy of their actions.

Historically, the development of the welfare states has followed a pattern reflected in this book's argument: social protection precedes state intervention. Welfare has not been imposed from above, but constructed on the foundations of pre-existing systems. Douglas Ashford – whose analysis is strongly centred on state activity – describes the process in these terms:

> First, the liberal refuge of private or charitable assistance proved totally inadequate. Second, the private insurers learned . . . that many serious social problems exceeded the capacity of actuarially sound insurance. Third . . . professional groups were gradually co-opted into national social security programmes. Fourth, the agricultural sector . . . received the protection of the state . . . before substantial aid went to urban dwellers.[282]

The main qualification to make about this description concerns the third point. Professional groups were 'co-opted', but that term might be taken at face value to imply that their schemes were simply swallowed up by state schemes. In France, professional groups retained a complex system of 'special' and 'complementary' regimes. In Germany, higher income earners were left out of basic coverage. In Sweden, schemes became 'selective by occupational experience'.[283] 'Co-option' depended on a process of bargaining and compromise, but it did not lead to the extinction of existing arrangements.

The pattern of development has not been the same in every country, and in some developing and recently developed nations there has been a conscious and deliberate attempt to emulate the welfare states by the introduction of state-sponsored schemes. India made a determined effort in the period after independence to introduce insurance coverage, though the intermittent nature of formal employment in many parts of

---

281 Baldwin (1990); Esping-Andersen (1996).
282 D. Ashford (1986) *The emergence of the welfare states*, Oxford: Blackwell, p. 107.
283 S. Ringen (1989) *The possibility of politics*, Oxford: Clarendon Press, p. 13.

the country hindered progress.[284] Jordan introduced a national insurance scheme, from almost no foundation, in the course of less than ten years.[285] (Jordan has also, by an interesting coincidence, been able to reduce poverty, inequality and infant mortality since that process began, despite a fall in national income.)[286] These are much closer than the major industrial countries to an ideal type of welfare state imposed from above by government, though there is every reason to defend the legitimacy of their action.

III.2.d.ii   *There is more than one kind of welfare state.*

The idea of the welfare state is an ambiguous one. I have used the term to refer to the formal institution of social protection, but involvement of this kind has become so extensive, and so widespread, that the term 'welfare state' does little to distinguish modern industrial states from each other. Although the idea refers to welfare provided by the state, it is also used to refer to an ideal model of provision. In this ideal, welfare is provided comprehensively, for every citizen. Asa Briggs, in a classic essay on the British welfare state, identified three principal elements. These were a guarantee of minimum standards, including a minimum income; social protection in the event of insecurity; and the provision of services at the best level possible.[287] This has become identified, in practice, with the 'institutional' model of welfare described first by Wilensky and Lebeaux,[288] and developed by Titmuss:[289] the key elements are social protection, and the provision of welfare services on the basis of right.

This model is closely associated with the British welfare state; other countries have represented the welfare state in different ways. Sweden can be seen as another ideal form of 'welfare state', offering institutional care in the sense that it offers universal minima to its citizens.[290] It goes further than the British welfare state in its commitment to social equality.

---

284 S. Hasan (1969) 'Social security in India: limited resources, unlimited needs', in S. Jenkins, *Social security in international perspective*, New York: Columbia University Press; J. Midgley (1984) *Social security, inequality and the Third World*, Chichester: Wiley.

285 A. Ata (1987) 'Jordan', in J. Dixon (ed.) *Social welfare in the Middle East*, Beckenham: Croom Helm.

286 United Nations Development Program (1997) *Human Development Report*, Oxford: Oxford University Press, pp. 8, 73, 162.

287 A. Briggs (1961) 'The welfare state in historical perspective', *European Journal of Sociology*, 2: 221–258.

288 H. Wilensky and C. Lebeaux (1965) *Industrial society and social welfare*, New York: Free Press.

289 Titmuss (1974).

290 S. Olsson (1987) 'Towards a transformation of the Swedish welfare state', in R. Morris, N. Gilbert and M. Sherer (eds) *Modern welfare states*, Brighton: Wheatsheaf.

Titmuss's 'institutional-redistributive' model, which combines the principles of comprehensive social equality with egalitarianism, can be seen as an idealized version of these objectives. Social protection is not necessarily associated with equality; the French and German systems offer differential protection according to one's position in the labour market. The Swedish system has many of the same characteristics.[291] However, the importance of equality – sometimes identified with 'solidarity', in the sense of organized co-operation – is considerable. The model of this is the 'solidaristic wage policy' advocated in the 1970s by the labour movement, which emphasized improving standards, limited differentials, and redistribution.[292] These policies are sometimes referred to as 'social-democratic';[293] they can equally be seen as socialistic in their emphasis on collective action and egalitarian redistribution. There has however been a liberal backlash against these policies in Sweden, which has attempted to distance welfare provision from their principles.[294]

Germany provides a third approach to welfare.[295] The post-war German settlement was based on the idea of a 'social state', sometimes rendered as a 'social market economy'. The first, central principle was that social welfare would most effectively be furthered through economic development, and that the structure of social services had to reflect that. This principle is represented most clearly in the close relationship of services to one's position in the labour market; social benefits are earnings-related, and those without work records may find they are not covered for important contingencies. Less clear, but probably even more important, is the general concern to ensure that public expenditure on welfare is directly compatible with the need for economic development and growth. Second, the German economy, and the welfare system, developed through a corporatist structure.[296] This principle was developed by Bismarck from existing mutual aid associations, and remained the basis for social protection subsequently.[297] Social insurance, which covers the costs of health, some social care and much of the income maintenance system, is managed by a system of independent funds. Third, there is a strong emphasis on the Catholic principle of

291 S. Ringen (1989), p. 13.

292 D. Robinson (1972) *Solidaristic wage policy in Sweden*, Paris: OECD.

293 Gould (1996).

294 A. Gould (1993) 'The end of the middle way?', in C. Jones (ed.) *New perspectives on the welfare state in Europe*, London: Routledge.

295 Clasen and Freeman (1994); R. Lawson (1996) 'Germany: maintaining the middle way', in George and Taylor-Gooby (1996).

296 G.A. Ritter (1983) *Social welfare in Germany and Britain*, Leamington Spa: Berg.

297 G. Rimlinger (1971) *Welfare policy and industrialisation*, New York: John Wiley; J. Alber (1986) 'Germany', in Flora (1986); E. Rosenhaft (1994) 'The historical development of German social policy', in Clasen and Freeman (1994).

'subsidiarity'.[298] This principle means different things to different people, but is taken in Germany to mean both that services should be decentralized or independently managed, and that the level of state intervention should be residual – that is, limited to circumstances which are not adequately covered in other ways. Higher earners are not covered by the main social insurance system, but are left to make their own arrangements. The key characteristics of the German system are represented by Lenoir, by contrast with the welfare state of the UK, as socio-professional social insurance; a decentralized administration; being financed by social contributions on salary, subject to a ceiling, with proportionate social benefits; and obligatory only for people below the ceiling.[299] This represents a fundamentally different approach to the rights-based, universal 'welfare state'.

> History shapes law and institutions appropriate to each nation, but which always refers to one logic or another: social insurance based on solidarity between members of professional groups, or national social security founded on solidarity between citizens.[300]

A different approach again is offered by the United States. The US is often presented as a liberal, residual welfare state, but the situation is more complex. The system is federal, and although the interventions of state governments have tended to be limited, there are exceptions: two states, Minnesota and Hawaii, currently have state-wide health systems. The initiatives of the federal government, which have been restricted by law and convention, have often been developed as special 'programs' rather than as developed services. There is a patchwork of provision, which varies considerably according to locality and the circumstances of the person in need. The system is, then, pluralistic rather than residual; although the role of government tends to be limited, there are areas of welfare provision (like coverage of health care and education) which are relatively wide-ranging. There is, equally, a very substantial level of provision on a corporate, occupational basis.[301] Klass describes the dominant model of welfare as a form of 'decentralised social altruism';[302] collective action is extensive, but it is localized, communitarian and based in narrowly defined circumstances.

---

298 D. Jarré (1991) 'Subsidiarity in social services in Germany', *Social Policy and Administration*, 25 (3): 211–217.

299 D. Lenoir (1994) *L'Europe sociale*, Paris: Editions la Découverte.

300 B. Majnoni d'Intignano (1993) *La Protection sociale*, Paris: Editions de Fallois.

301 D. Stoesz and H. Karger (1991) 'The corporatisation of the US welfare state', *Journal of Social Policy*, 20 (2): 157–172.

302 G. Klass (1985) 'Explaining America and the welfare state', *British Journal of Political Science*, 15: 427–450.

III.2.d.iii   The welfare states elude classification.

Gøsta Esping-Andersen has classified the main welfare regimes as being social democratic, liberal-residual, and corporatist.[303] Social democratic regimes, most nearly represented here by Sweden, have a commitment to welfare, with universal rights. The corporatist regimes, represented by Germany, are characterized by state influence in provision, rather than the direct provision of services by the state itself. Liberal regimes, represented by the United States, are residual, limiting the role of the state and depending to the greatest degree on the economic market. This kind of classification is useful – it helps to show something of the range and diversity of schemes adopted by democratic governments. At the same time, there are important reservations to make about it (▶ Method); none of these welfare states can be represented as a consistent, monolithic system with a single approach to policy.

Esping-Andersen's classification is one of several. Leibfried, for example, distinguishes the Scandinavian welfare states, including Sweden, Norway and Denmark; Bismarckian systems, mainly Germany and Austria; Anglo-Saxon countries, including the US, UK and Australia; and the 'Latin Rim' of Spain, Portugal, Greece and Italy, which offer 'rudimentary' welfare.[304] Palme, writing about pensions, distinguishes four models: 'residual', the model in the UK, US and France; 'citizenship', represented by Australia and Denmark, which extend rights to everyone; 'work-merit', represented by Germany, in which welfare is related directly to a person's position in the labour market; and 'institutional' welfare, represented by Sweden, which offers benefits as of right, at a high level.[305] Each of these classifications is initially plausible on its own terms – and each puts some countries together in different combinations; there is no agreement on the basis of the different categories. This happens, in part, because some countries are particularly difficult to classify: Denmark, Ireland[306] and Australia[307] occupy different places in the literature, according to the aspects of their systems which are identified. But it also happens, more fundamentally, because welfare systems are

---

303 Esping-Andersen (1990).

304 S. Leibfried (1991) *Towards a European welfare state?* Bremen: Zentrum für Sozialpolitik.

305 J. Palme (1990) 'Models of old-age pensions', in A. Ware and R. Goodin (eds) *Needs and welfare*, London: Sage.

306 E. McLaughlin (1993) 'Ireland: Catholic corporatism', in A. Cochrane and J. Clarke (eds) *Comparing welfare states*, London: Sage; M. Cousins (1997) 'Ireland's place in the worlds of welfare capitalism', *Journal of European Social Policy*, 7 (3): 223–235.

307 B. Cass and J. Freeland (1994) 'Social security and full employment in Australia', in J. Hills, J. Ditch and H. Glennerster (eds) *Beveridge and social security*, Oxford: Clarendon Press; F. Castles (1994) 'Comparing the Australian and Scandinavian welfare states', *Scandinavian Political Studies*, 17 (1): 31–46.

complex and diverse. In many comparisons, there are likely to be both consonances and differences between the systems which are being compared; the identification of family resemblances between different countries depends heavily on interpretation.

The theoretical framework laid out in this book identifies only the similarities between welfare states; it does not explain their diversity. The development of particular forms of welfare depends on a range of historical, social and political factors which are distinctive to particular welfare states, and a general theory cannot address them. Peter Baldwin makes the case that different types of explanation are needed for different problems. Social explanations address broad issues of relationships and interest formation; political, state-centred interpretations of the welfare states address issues of formulation and implementation.[308] The approaches are complementary: both help to give a fuller understanding of the subject.

---

308 Baldwin (1990), p. 47.

III.3

SOCIAL POLICY

III.3 Welfare is promoted and maintained through social policy.

The promotion of welfare
III.3.a   *Social policies should aim to enhance welfare.*
III.3.a.i   Social policy is a moral activity.
III.3.a.ii   There is a moral duty to enhance welfare.
III.3.a.iii   Social policy should enhance both personal and social welfare.

Functions of social policy
III.3.b   *Social policies serve many purposes.*
III.3.b.i   The focus is both personal and social.
III.3.b.ii   Social policy cannot adequately be described in ideological terms.

Legitimate and illegitimate activity
III.3.c   *Social protection is not always illegitimate; but nor is it always legitimate.*
III.3.c.i   Social services can be beneficial or destructive.
III.3.c.ii   They can be liberating, or oppressive.
III.3.c.iii   Social policy must be judged in its context.

The promotion of welfare

III.3.a   Social policies should aim to enhance welfare.

The 'social policy' of a government is the set of measures and approaches it adopts in relation to social protection and the provision of welfare. The suggestion that social policy should increase welfare may seem so obvious as to be hardly worth discussing: the general principle that states have the duty to promote welfare has been accepted for centuries. The central argument is, simply enough, that welfare is a good, and that government exists to do good things for people; other supplementary arguments are based on obligations towards people in need, and on the rights of citizens.

There are, however, several grounds on which the proposition might be objected to. There is a view that social policy itself cannot be a legitimate activity, a position which has already been discussed. It is possible to argue that social policy is not necessarily about welfare at all, and might have different aims altogether. And the case may be made that social policy should not enhance welfare, but may justifiably detract from it.

The argument that social policy is not about welfare has more substance than is immediately obvious, because social policy is not just about welfare. Social policy is a moral activity (▶ II.3.d), but what is right is not necessarily what is good (▶ I.4.b.ii). We educate children in the hope that it will benefit them, but if it does not, that is not a very good reason for not doing it. We educate them because it is the right thing to do. Even if we thought it would make them miserable instead, it would not be a good reason not to educate them.

The argument that social policy may justifiably detract from welfare is an important one. Social policy can use sticks, as well as carrots. This occurs most usually in the context of a conflict of interests: that a person or group has to suffer for the benefit of other people. Behaviour which is thought of as undesirable – like discrimination, insanitary behaviour, marital discord, unregulated trade, even being bad neighbours – can be curbed.

III.3.a.i Social policy is a moral activity.

The core element in these arguments is that social policy involves some kind of moral judgement. This proposition is not self-evident, because although parts of the activity are concerned with moral issues, parts are not. The provision of food or housing are not seen as moral activities: why should welfare be different? The answer rests in the nature of policy – the idea that governments take decisions about the nature and pattern of provision. When the same is true of food or housing, they become moral issues, too. The effect of policy decisions is that governments make a choice to affect outcomes or methods. By doing so, they accept some responsibility for those outcomes or methods. (This position is not distinctive to government. If a commercial firm or cartel has sufficient power to affect outcomes and procedures, such as the operation of a whole market, it takes on moral responsibilities, too.)

There is a corollary to this argument: moral responsibility extends beyond the scope of deliberate policy. Any social action has the potential to activate moral principles, and the deliberate intention to act morally is not required before it happens. Isolated actions become precedents; actions in particular cases become general rules, because of the need to act consistently. The acceptance of responsibility for injury to soldiers in wartime – a policy which it would be difficult for any government to resist morally – was at the root of many policies for disabled people: in the UK, the Blind Persons' Act of 1920,[309] or in the US the establishment of the Veterans' Administration, which provides medical care for nearly a tenth of the population.[310] Once liability for soldiers is accepted, it is difficult to resist the acceptance of liability for civilians who are in essential occupations; liability for some civilians, and not others, implies an invidious distinction; and so it goes. This is one of the reasons for the progressive expansion of responsibility of governments.

III.3.a.ii *There is a moral duty to enhance welfare.*

Morality has been closely identified with welfare: the basis of the utilitarian argument is that morals are based in actions which lead to people being better off. There is a general moral obligation to improve welfare. This obligation is strongest to those to whom one is closest sccially; it weakens as people become more socially distant (▶ I.3.a.i).

   This is not, of course, the only moral obligation that people are subject to, and there are many cases where welfare is outweighed by other considerations. Criminal justice is generally founded, not just on welfare, but on the idea of punishment – the returning of evil for evil. But there is also a welfare approach, geared to the reintegration and rehabilitation of the offender in society. Welfare considerations apply, then, even where other contradictory principles run counter to promotion of welfare.

III.3.a.iii *Social policy should enhance both personal and*
social welfare.

Welfare is not a simple, monolithic concept, and the statement that social policies should enhance welfare is potentially ambiguous. Personal welfare can be pursued to the detriment of social welfare, and vice versa.

   Both personal and social well-being are good things (by definition), and both are included in the general proposition that government should try to do good things. But there are additional principles at work. In the case of personal welfare, the central argument is based in individual rights. People who do not experience well-being as individuals are probably not going to experience well-being at all.

   Social welfare is both an aspect of personal welfare, because people are part of a society, and a form of well-being in its own right. The welfare of a society encompasses social integration (the opposite of exclusion) and economic development, which is also a precondition for welfare. A

---

309 J. Brown (1984) *The Disability Income System*, London: Policy Studies Institute, pp. 15–16.
310 S. Jonas (1986) *Health care delivery in the US*, New York: Springer.

failure to consider social welfare, then, can undermine some important aspects of personal welfare.

Functions of social policy

III.3.b   Social policies serve many purposes.

Social policy, and the social services – the organized institutions of the welfare states – serve many more purposes than the provision of welfare. Because social services relate to the conduct of individuals and groups, they can be adapted to a range of policies. In a previous book, I outlined six basic categories: providing for needs, remedying disadvantage, changing behaviour, developing potential, maintaining circumstances and producing disadvantage.[311] Each of these categories has been discussed at some point of this argument. Only providing for needs and developing potential are unequivocally committed to the enhancement of welfare. The maintenance of social circumstances may serve to protect people, and to make them secure, but it may also trap them in unsatisfactory conditions. Remedying disadvantage is about redistribution: it pursues the advantage of some at the disadvantage of others. This will usually enhance welfare, though I have noted some exceptions. Producing disadvantage is similarly about redistribution, though the emphasis here falls more squarely on making some people worse off.

III.3.b.i   The focus is both personal and social.

Social policies can be addressed to individuals or to social groups. Table 2 summarizes the different dimensions. The needs of individuals are met through personal provision; the needs of society through instrumental measures like economic development or education for employment. Maintenance for individuals is achieved by social insurance, or other forms of social protection; maintenance for a society implies policies for 'reproduction' (▶ I.2.b.iv), ensuring that one generation succeeds another, that children are socialized, that the economy is stable and that traditions and codes are continued. Remedying the disadvantage of individuals can be done by compensating people for their poor position – as in compensation for disability, or compensatory education – or seeking to change them through treatment or cure of a condition. Remedying disadvantage in a society is done through policies for equality or social justice. Lastly, there is the production of disadvantage, most obviously through punishing individuals who have broken rules. At the social level, disadvantage has been produced deliberately by regimes which have wished to foster social division: an example was the apartheid

---

311 P. Spicker (1993) *Poverty and social security: concepts and principles*, London: Routledge.

Table 2 *Individual and collective welfare*

	Individual welfare	Collective welfare
Provision for needs	Humanitarian provision	Economic development
Maintenance of social circumstances	Social insurance	Reproduction
Changing behaviour	Rewards; incentives; treatment	Social control
Development of potential	Development of individual capacities	Solidarity; social cohesion and integration
Remedying disadvantage	Compensation; cure	Equality; social justice
The production of disadvantage	Punishment	Social division

regime in South Africa, which distinguished welfare provision for recipients according to their racial status.

III.3.b.ii *Social policy cannot adequately be described in ideological terms.*

The language in which social policy is discussed rarely gives a sense of
the diversity and complexity of social policy in practice. Social policy,
and the welfare states, combine some politically sensitive and highly
charged issues with a vast hinterland of miscellaneous measures, and a
level of practical detail which no one can really hope to master; special-
ists in the subject tend to focus on limited areas within the field as a
whole. People need to simplify – to find a formula which will help them
to make sense of the tangled whole. Much of the commentary on the
subject is driven, in consequence, by ideological perceptions of the field.
An ideology is a set of interrelated values and beliefs; ideologies of
welfare are often represented as pre-constructed systems of views and
opinions.[312] Even if people do not buy all their ideas in bulk, discourse
on welfare is often channelled into predictable, well-worn ruts. Debates
at the political level are reflected in the pattern of popular discourse,
and opinions are expressed in terms of a limited set of 'moral reper-
toires'.[313] The discussion of 'welfare' in the US, for example, commonly
focuses on financial benefits and dependency, not on social security or
health care;[314] social welfare in France is dominated by the concept of

---

312 J. Clarke, A. Cochrane and C. Smart (1987) *Ideologies of welfare*, London:
Hutchinson; V. George and P. Wilding (1994) *Welfare and ideology*, Hemel
Hempstead: Harvester Wheatsheaf.
313 H. Dean (1998) 'Popular paradigms and welfare values', *Critical Social
Policy*, 55, 18 (2): 131–156.
314 S. Schram (1995) *Words of welfare*, Minneapolis: University of Minnesota
Press.

'solidarity';[315] discourse in the UK, fifty years after the abolition of the Poor Law, is still dominated by the question of what the welfare state does for the poor.[316]

One of the most important insights to be gained from the preceding sections is the understanding that social policy cannot be described adequately in these ideological terms. It is neither exclusively benevolent, nor unremittingly illiberal. This should not be surprising: social policy is complex, and the effects of policy may be contradictory or ambiguous.

Legitimate and illegitimate activity

III.3.c Social protection is not always illegitimate; but nor is it always legitimate.

Much of the debate about social welfare begins from the question of whether government intervention can ever be legitimate. This is the position, in different ways, of critics on both right and left of the political spectrum. On one hand, there are ultra-liberals, who argue that any government intervention is coercive, and liable to disrupt desirable social processes;[317] on the other, there are Marxists and quasi-Marxists who argue that welfare states are fatally compromised by their role in an exploitative, capitalist system of economic production.[318] Both of these positions are deeply flawed – they are based in inadequate, distorted views of society, misunderstandings of the political process, and fallacious accounts of the development of welfare – but I have discussed them at length in previous work,[319] and I am not able to deal with them in the course of this argument without serious digression.

It is clear enough that social policy can be a legitimate activity. If legitimate governments pursue the welfare of their citizens (▶ III.2.a), if the object of government is the welfare of the people (▶ III.2.a.i), and if governments have to protect the rights of their citizens (▶ III.2.b.ii), social protection is a legitimate concern of government. It is arguably the most legitimate concern many of them have. The case for it in these terms is at

---

315 P. Spicker (1998) 'Exclusion and citizenship in France', in M. Mullard and S. Lee (eds) *The politics of social policy in Europe*, Aldershot: Edward Elgar.

316 S. Becker (1997) *Responding to poverty*, London: Longman.

317 H. Spencer (1851) *Social statics*, London: Murray, 1984.

318 E.g. J. Saville (1975) 'The welfare state: an historical approach', in E. Butterworth and R. Holman, *Social welfare in modern Britain*, Glasgow: Fontana; N. Poulantzas (1978) *State, power, socialism*, London: NLB; C. Offe (1984) *Contradictions of the welfare state*, London: Hutchinson.

319 E.g. M. Mullard and P. Spicker (1998) *Social policy in a changing society*, London: Routledge.

least as strong, and perhaps stronger, than the case for foreign policy or defence, which liberals accept as legitimate functions of the state.[320]

The converse of this is that governments can act improperly, and there are several examples of governments doing evil things through their social policies. Social policies can be racialist, inhumane, even murderous. In Nazi Germany, social policy was a primary means through which ideas of race and nation were realized, with a powerful emphasis on eugenics. The 1933 law to prevent hereditarily sick offspring provided for compulsory sterilization of a range of hereditary conditions, including Huntington's chorea, blindness, deafness, physical malformation, and feeble-mindedness, as well as dealing with people with other less obviously inherited disorders, including epilepsy, schizophrenia, manic depression, and severe alcoholism.[321] Grunberger notes that 'By the outbreak of the war, 375,000 people (including 200,000 feeble minded, 73,000 schizophrenics, 57,000 epileptics and nearly 30,000 alcoholics) had been sterilised, the vast majority of them involuntarily.'[322] Ultimately, this programme was linked in with medical killing, which Weindling describes as 'a pilot scheme for the holocaust'.[323]

Social policy can be legitimate or illegitimate. The important question to address – a question which, in different ways, is disregarded both by the New Right and by Marxists – is whether it is legitimate in the circumstances in which it is applied.

III.3.c.i Social services can be beneficial or destructive.

The idea that social services can be beneficial is fundamental to much of the argument of this book, and it does not really require extensive examination at this stage. If the effects of exchange, collective action or pooled risk are beneficial, then so are the actions of social services.

The idea that social services can be destructive, by contrast, has been very little considered. If social services have the power to change social relationships, they must have the power to change relationships negatively as well as positively. Destruction implies, not just that they can change relationships, but that in certain cases they can extinguish them. A contentious example is the question of whether social policy undermines relationships in the family. The accusation that it might has commonly been made, both from the political left (who have condemned

---

320 E.g. Nozick (1974); N.P. Barry (1987) *The new right*, Beckenham: Croom Helm.

321 P. Weindling (1989) *Health, race and German politics between national unification and Nazism 1870–1945*, Cambridge: Cambridge University Press, pp. 522–525.

322 R. Grunberger (1974) *A social history of the Third Reich*, Harmondsworth: Penguin, p. 288.

323 Weindling (1989), p. 548.

policies like the household means test for its effect on family support)[324] and the political right (who have argued that benefits have led to a massive increase in illegitimacy and abandonment of families by irresponsible fathers).[325] Difficult as these claims are to resolve, because they refer to issues with multiple causes, they are basically empirical questions. There is some evidence that unemployment and economic marginality disturb family relationships,[326] but it has not been possible to distinguish the influence of benefits within this pattern. There is a related moral issue – whether the structure of social policies should penalize people for adopting socially valued behaviour, or reward them for doing things which are disvalued. There is some reason to suspect that social protection is being blamed for the effects of the conditions it is designed to alleviate.

There is much better evidence of social policy acting destructively. At the turn of the century, the predominant belief relating to mental disorder was that it stemmed from 'degeneracy', or biological inadequacy. Degeneracy was identified with mental retardation, but it was held to be the source of a range of social problems, including mental illness, crime, illegitimacy, and dependency on welfare.[327] Part of the response to this was eugenics, or selective breeding, fulfilled in the policies of Fascism. The eugenics movement had an extensive influence in other areas, however; the terms on which people were incarcerated in institutions, and the types of institutions they were placed in, were directly influenced by eugenic ideas. Mental institutions, which held both mentally ill people and those with learning disabilities, were built to contain people, not to cure them. The purpose of the institutions was to isolate degenerates from the community, and that is what they did – cutting people off from society, so that they had no contact or relationships outside the closed institution.[328] The legacy of this policy, actively pursued in the 1920s and 1930s, continues to be the source of the problems of institutions in the present day.[329]

---

324 M. Bruce (1968) *The coming of the welfare state*, London: Batsford, pp. 273–274.

325 N. Dennis and G. Erdos (1992) *Families without fatherhood*, London: Institute of Economic Affairs.

326 R. Lampard (1994) 'An examination of the relationship between marital dissolution and unemployment', in D. Gallie, C. Marsh and C. Vogler (eds) *Social change and the experience of unemployment*, Oxford: Oxford University Press.

327 D. Wright and A. Digby (eds) (1996) *From idiocy to mental deficiency*, London: Routledge.

328 W. Wolfensberger (1975) *The origin and nature of our institutional models*, Syracuse, NY: Human Policy Press; D. Wright and A. Digby (eds) (1996) *From idiocy to mental deficiency*, London: Routledge.

329 D. Cohen (1988) *Forgotten millions*, London: Paladin; K. Jones (1993) *Asylums and after*, London: Athlone.

Social services can, then, be destructive of social relationships. The examples considered here and in the previous section indicate that they may even be designed to be destructive.

III.3.c.ii *They can be liberating, or oppressive.*

The argument that social policy can deny freedom should be familiar. If action to benefit others restricts their choice of action – even the choice to do things which are damaging to themselves or others – freedom has been restricted. Social welfare is often paternalistic – putting people's welfare before their independence of action. Soyer argues for the 'right to fail'; people need to be able to go wrong if they are ever to learn what is right.[330] From both left and right, intervention through social welfare meets with a chorus of disapproval. To the right wing, it represents an unwarranted interference in people's liberty;[331] to the left, it reveals welfare as a mechanism of control and oppression.[332]

These criticisms underestimate the extent to which social policies can enhance freedom. Freedom is a triadic relationship, involving not only the absence of restraint, but the power to act, and the ability to choose (▶ II.2.c.i). Resources are crucial for freedom, because without resources people are unable to exercise choice. Poverty denies freedom, and the relief of poverty protects people against it. (I had a disagreement on this point once with a lawyer. 'Nonsense', he told me. 'Poverty doesn't have anything to do with freedom.'

'Do you think', I asked, 'that freedom means freedom to choose?'
'Yes.'
'And people with less money are less able to choose than others?'
'Yes.'
'So people with less money must be less free.'
At which he stiffened, and said, 'I'm not having you foist your crackpot ideas on me', before marching off. It never happens like that in Plato.)

There is a fine moral balance to be struck. The same policies can, in different circumstances, have contradictory effects. Intervention is permitted which is likely to increase freedom. Compulsory education gives people the independence and power to act; if it is not compulsory, those likely to be denied the benefits of education are precisely those most likely in the future to be denied other freedoms. Compulsory detention for psychiatric patents has as its objective the restoration of a person to a fully functioning, autonomous state. These interventions

---

330 D. Soyer (1975) 'The right to fail', in F. McDermott (ed.) *Self-determination in social work*, London: Routledge and Kegan Paul.

331 E.g. F. Hayek (1944) *The road to serfdom*, London: Routledge and Kegan Paul.

332 E.g. H. Dean (1991) *Social security and social control*, London: Routledge.

cease to be justifiable when they infringe on freedom: education becomes indoctrination, or compulsory detention becomes institutionalization. These measures can increase freedom, but they also have, at the same time, the potential to reduce it.

III.3.c.iii Social policy must be judged in its context.

Policies cannot be judged *in vacuo*. If the same policy can be used for good or ill, it is not necessarily the content of the policy which determines its legitimacy. Intentions are clearly important: there is not much wrong with encouraging children to be fit, but that does not extend to the Hitler Youth. Equally, social policies are sometimes based on difficult choices, which justify means that might otherwise seem illegitimate: examples are the isolation of the carriers of infectious disease, or the provision of contraceptives to young children.

The outcomes of policy have to be considered. The field which social policy deals with is complex, and policies commonly generate a range of unintended effects, both positive and negative, which have to be considered before a policy can meaningfully be assessed. Well-intentioned policies can prove disastrously harmful: 'community care', the discharge of psychiatric patients into an unsupported environment, springs to mind.[333] It is more difficult to argue that policies which are manifestly ill-intentioned may still have some beneficial effects, because it sounds like a defence of the indefensible: clearly, the policies of Nazism were very popular, partly because of the economic benefits they generated, but it is hardly a justification for the process.

---

333 P. Bean and P. Mounser (1993) *Discharged from mental hospitals*, Basingstoke: Macmillan, ch. 2; A. Lurigio and D. Lewis (1993) 'Worlds that fail: a longitudinal study of urban mental patients', in P. Baker, L. Anderson and D. Dorn (eds) *Social problems*, New York: Wadsworth; J. Ritchie (chair) (1994) *Report of the inquiry into the care and treatment of Christopher Clunis*, London: HMSO.

III.4

STATE ACTION

III.4 The welfare states have a wide range of options through which social policies can be pursued.

The state and social policy
- *III.4.a*   *States can do tnings which other associations cannot.*
- III.4.a.i   States establish rules.
- III.4.a.ii   Governments coerce.
- III.4.a.iii   Governments subsidize and provide.
- III.4.a.iv   Governments persuade.
- III.4.a.v   Governments plan.

Provision by the state
- *III.4.b*   *The state operates differently from the market.*
- III.4.b.i   The supply and demand for services provided by the state are interdependent.
- III.4.b.ii   The provision of services is not determined by cost.
- III.4.b.iii   State provision cannot be efficient.
- III.4.b.iv   There are other reasons for provision by the state.

The production of welfare
- *III.4.c*   *The welfare states have come to set the terms on which social protection is delivered.*
- III.4.c.i   Welfare is delivered through many channels.
- III.4.c.ii   The welfare states build on other forms of social protection.
- III.4.c.iii   The action of the state must be seen in the context of existing provision.
- III.4.c.iv   The promotion of welfare requires the interweaving of state provision with other forms of solidaristic support.

Welfare strategies
- *III.4.d*   *The approach to policy affects its nature.*
- III.4.d.i   Outcomes can be realized in many ways.

III.4.d.ii   Methods and processes influence outcomes.
III.4.d.iii   The choice of methods cannot fully be distinguished from
              the purposes of policy.

Assessing social policy
    III.4.e   *Welfare strategies can be assessed by common criteria.*

The state and social policy

III.4.a States can do things which other associations cannot.

Much of the argument of the first part of this book was based in the
networks of relationships which characterize modern societies, including
both informal networks and formal associations. States are like formal
associations, and they can do many things which other formal associations can do, but they also have a capacity for action beyond that of
other organizations. The core of this capacity lies in legitimate authority,
which makes it morally possible for governments to bind and direct the
actions of others.

III.4.a.i   States establish rules.

A legal system, Hart argues, needs two types of rules. Primary rules are
the rules by which laws can be made: they include rules of recognition,
change and adjudication. Rules of recognition make it possible to
identify what is a rule, and what its status is in law. Rules of change
provide procedures by which laws can be introduced, changed or
adapted. Rules of adjudication determine the ways in which rules can be
judged to apply. Secondary rules are the substantive laws.[334]

The most basic role of the state is the establishment of the rules under
which services operate. Beyond this, states commonly move, through
substantive laws, to regulate the patterns of behaviour of organizations.
This is done through a combination of legal restraints, prohibitions and
conditional requirements, generally supplemented by some of the other
measures described in following sections. Although the power of the
state is often seen as coercive, and states can coerce individual citizens,
states are not generally in a position to coerce organizations, because
formal organizations can be dissolved rather than comply. The process is
more typically one in which government agencies try to persuade, educate, encourage, push, threaten, bluster or browbeat agencies into doing
the kinds of things that the government wants them to do. In other
words, it is a matter of politics rather than of law, and in this respect the
actions of the state are not necessarily distinguishable from those of other
social institutions.

---

334 H.L.A. Hart (1961) *The concept of law*, Oxford: Oxford University Press.

III.4.a.ii   Governments coerce.

The most basic tools which governments have to change behaviour are prohibition and coercion: they can pass a law which says that people must not do something (like performing surgical operations when not qualified to do so, dropping litter, or taking drugs), or that they must do something (like support their families, clean the street outside their homes, or send their child to school). The existence of this kind of law is very much taken for granted, so much so that it would be possible to suppose that the action of government is always coercive; voluntary exhortations carry the veiled implication that if they do not work, stronger measures may follow. But there are reservations to make. Given the choice, governments in the liberal democracies are often disinclined to use coercive forms of law. Prohibition and coercion do not always work; some laws are openly flouted, others are bent (like vehicle speed limits). Governments have learned to use prohibitions, not in the expectation that they will be obeyed, but in the hope that they will make a difference to behaviour. An example is the prohibition, in Sweden, of hitting children. No one seriously believes that parents will stop hitting children completely because a law has been passed; but the law acts as a way of helping to change attitudes, and as a way of ensuring that parents who damage children seriously cannot try to excuse themselves by saying (as they do in other countries) 'I didn't mean to do it so hard'.

Social protection may involve elements of compulsion. Some of the issues have been considered in previous sections: compulsion may be employed to avoid undesirable actions (▶ I.4.c.i), to impose moral action (▶ I.4.c), to avoid the problems of the 'free rider' (▶ I.3.b.iii(1)), in the imposition of a regulatory framework (▶ III.4.a.i), or in the imposition of minimum standards. The acknowledgement that governments coerce in such circumstances may seem to concede one of the principal criticisms made by ultra-liberals: that state action, whether it is meant for good or ill, is necessarily an infringement of individual liberty.[335] That is a misrepresentation of the issues. Liberty is not licence: coercion by the state may restrict activities which are not permitted. Coercion may enhance liberty; this is a central argument for compulsory education, and for many other minimum standards, such as standards in health and housing. Coercion can be used to protect some people from the actions, or inactions, of others: employers may have to be compelled to offer facilities for their employees, producers to offer minimum standards to consumers, and parents can be compelled to take action on behalf of their children. And the coercive nature of the action may not result from the state, but from society. The image of the state as uniquely coercive is misleading: organizations (like industrial firms or unions), religious bodies, neighbourhoods and families also coerce people. All that govern-

---

335 Hayek (1944).

ment does is to formalize it. The central moral issue about coercion – an issue which is often regrettably overlooked – is not whether it should ever take place, but whether the coercion is legitimate.

III.4.a.iii Governments subsidize and provide.

Governments may also intervene through measures intended to provide services. They can do this in three main ways: provision, purchasing of services, and subsidy and incentive. Provision means that states provide services themselves. Public housing, national health services or state education are obvious examples. Purchasing services implies that the state accepts responsibility for ensuring provision – and that, in the last resort, the state will be bound itself to provide – but that the service can be obtained from another agency. The basic argument for purchasing, rather than providing, is that independent services are better able to provide services than the state is. This applies in circumstances where competition drives prices down, requiring producers to be more efficient, but it does not always apply, and there are circumstances where states can achieve economies denied to the private sector. The private sector can duplicate facilities; it can shore up prices artificially, especially where entry to the market by other providers is difficult; it can suffer diseconomies of scale. This is most notably the case in the provision of health services, where publicly provided services have proved to be cheaper than the private sector.[336]

Subsidy consists of a financial inducement to act in a particular way, in the form of a contribution towards revenue or reduction in costs. This can be designed as a reward for certain kinds of behaviour, as a compensation for costs (as in the case of subsidies for child care), or as an incentive to undertake different types of action, a point which will be returned to shortly. Subsidies change the conditions under which markets operate, and they are a key method of shifting patterns of behaviour in desired directions.

III.4.a.iv Governments persuade.

Altering patterns of behaviour seems, at first, to be easy: all one has to do is to pass a law. The reality is very different. People can often be directed to do things they were going to do anyway, like having fewer babies, working for pay or continuing their education. People are much less eager to do things they were not going to do, and policies for natalism (to encourage the birth rate), encouraging women to return to the home, or giving up alcohol have not been conspicuously successful. Seriously radical policies, like the attempt to dissolve the Catholic Church in

---

336 OECD (1992) *The reform of health care*, Paris: OECD.

revolutionary France, or to abolish the institution of marriage in the Soviet Union, are unlikely to work, because people are not going to abandon long-established relationships and responsibilities overnight. Most measures which are taken by governments are necessarily taken at the margins, because a broader, wider-ranging approach to change risks being destructive or ineffective.

In many cases, change is attempted, not by coercion, but by persuasion. Propaganda, exhortation and directed education tend to be limited in their effectiveness, though there are some striking exceptions: the effect of health education in the US has had a notable effect in reducing the incidence of heart disease.

The primary persuasive measures used by governments are incentives and disincentives. Incentives are much misunderstood in the literature of social policy, and in popular discourse. The assumption is that if people are paid to do something, they will be inclined to do it, and that if they are not paid, they will not.[337] This is a confusion between two different kinds of argument: arguments about psychological responses to stimuli, and arguments about economics. The psychological argument, taken on its own, is a good one: people who do things in response to certain stimuli can often be relied on to do them again when the stimuli are repeated. This means that those people who respond to financial inducements will often do so again. It does not mean that everyone will respond in the same way to the same stimulus.

The economic argument is more complex: it has three component elements. The first is that what people do in aggregate is predictable, in a way that what they do as individuals is not. When people are taken in aggregate, differences tend to cancel each other out, so that what results is an 'average' reaction. Often, it is a partial reaction: many people will not respond at all. That, however, is not a problem for a government which is trying to produce aggregate, rather than individual, effects.

Second, the behaviour of the average individual is based on the maximization of utility. This depends on a balance of factors; incentives have to be placed in context. People's behaviour depends on the relative costs and benefits of different options. An incentive changes relative costs or benefits; it does not override every other factor. Unemployment benefit is not an 'incentive' to be unemployed, any more than a death grant is an 'incentive' to become dead.

Third, and arguably most important, the economic analysis of incentives is based on marginal analysis. Marginal analysis focuses on how people respond to changes in circumstances which are already determined. The idea of 'elasticity' refers to the propensity of an aggregate population to respond to different conditions. Elasticity can, in some cases, be zero. No financial inducement is going to get people to chop their heads off or eat their grandmothers – at least, not in any large

---

337 C. Murray (1984) *Losing ground*, New York: Basic Books.

numbers. Economics may be a dismal science, but it is not as cynical as some people seem to assume. There is no assumption that people must respond directly to financial stimuli.

When governments offer incentives, what they are doing is trying to shift aggregate behaviour in a particular direction – trying to get more people into work, getting more people to provide residential homes, to get fewer people to travel by car, and so forth. What they are not doing (or what they should not be doing) is assuming that every single person will respond. Subsidies and tax reliefs are used as a means of altering the calculations made by a provider about financial viability of a project – the effect of increased revenue from a programme is to reduce costs. The same is true of disincentives: increasing the costs of an operation through taxation, or reducing benefits, will usually affect the marginal behaviour of some people (while penalizing others).

III.4.a.v   Governments plan.

Governments cannot usually determine outcomes directly, because too many effects of policy are unintended; but they can test policies, monitor them, and evaluate their outcomes. They can accept those policies which produce desired effects and reject others, until they begin to approximate the outcomes which they want to bring about. The government is not unique in its ability to plan and map social consequences, but it is uncertain that anyone else has an interest in doing so, and in practice the field has been left to governments – sometimes, admittedly, in conflict with other policies which are pulling in a different direction. The idea of 'corporatism', in which government proceeds in conjunction with a set of social partners who are drawn into the process of government, has flourished because this kind of arrangement seems overall to work at the behest of government.[338] But government does not need to direct the actions of the other agencies; it needs only to work around them, interrelating its activity with theirs, in order to produce something like the desired effect.

Provision by the state

III.4.b   The state operates differently from the market.

The state has a role as provider of last resort (▸ III.2.c.ii); its activities extend beyond that role (▸ III.2.c.iii); and, no less important, government may seek legitimately to further the principle of social justice (▸ III.2.c.iv). Each of these propositions implies that the state will, at least, be concerned with people who are excluded – with sectors of the population who are not otherwise covered. This has direct implications for welfare provision: the conditions under which the state provides welfare are

---

338 M. Harrison (1984) *Corporatism and the welfare state*, Aldershot: Gower.

different from the operation of welfare provision in non-state sectors, and in particular from the economic market. Economists usually apply to the state the criteria they would apply to an economic monopoly: on one hand, the lack of incentive to efficiency provided by competition, on the other the lack of choice and inability to exit on the part of consumers, which places them in a weak position when it comes to demanding improvements.[339] These criticisms are sometimes appropriate, but they are not the whole story; the criteria by which states operate are different from those of commercial concerns, and differences in motivation lead to differences in action.

III.4.b.i The supply and demand for services provided by the state are interdependent.

In a conventional economic analysis, the supply of services and the demand for them are treated largely as independent factors which can be brought into balance (or 'equilibrium') under certain conditions. When state social services are considered, however, supply and demand are interdependent. Partly, this may happen because the state determines both factors as a matter of policy: the demand for education is illustrative. It also happens because both supply and demand are a function of needs and aspirations, whether social or the aggregated needs of different people, and indeed of policy. They increase and diminish together; arguably they develop in parallel. The general experience of state services is that an increase in supply leads directly to an increase in demand, as people come to realize that a service is available which can meet their needs or wishes. Conversely, the effect of limiting the scope of services, or of strict rationing, is deterrence: demand may continue to outstrip supply, but the visible level of demand will usually fall, because people do not present their needs.

This leads, potentially, to some distortions in the response to need. Social protection can come to favour particular sectors or groups in the population, like civil servants or workers in public utilities. Governments which provide for certain needs can create a constituency of recipients with a vested interest in maintaining a relative advantage over non-recipients. (An example might be the special long-established privileges accorded to blind people relative to others with disabilities.) In extreme cases, this may take the form of clientelism.

III.4.b.ii The provision of services is not determined by cost.

Similarly, in a conventional economic analysis, the behaviour of the firm is primarily determined by the issue of profit. State expenditure on social

339 H. Glennerster (1997) *Paying for welfare: towards 2000*, Hemel Hempstead: Prentice-Hall, pp. 28–29.

services is constrained by total cost, which can be seen as analogous to the profit motive, but it is only a constraint, not the primary motivation; there is no strong incentive to minimize total costs. When governments do attempt to reduce expenditure in the name of economy, they generally face the 'paradox of targeting', that the effect of reducing coverage is to leave them with people with greater needs, and so to increase their average costs.[340] The role of the state as a provider of last resort means that when the relative costs of a service increase, an increasing residual demand is likely to be experienced by the state: for example, the effect of generally increasing costs in medical care may be to increase the demand for health care from the state.

Democratic governments do, however, have a common inducement to act in particular ways, and that is the pursuit of electoral advantage. This is usually seen positively: it is one of the principal routes through which governments are encouraged to respond to social needs.[341] But the electoral cycle can also limit the government's time-horizon, prompting short-term planning; the geographical dimensions of the electoral process might lead to distortion in the allocation of resources; the agendas which the government addresses are liable to be dominated by public and media attention, rather than the long-term interests of a society.[342]

III.4.b.iii   State provision cannot be efficient.

If the state has to make provision in the last resort, it has to provide for cases which commercial or mutual aid organizations would not provide for. These are liable to be people with lower resources, greater needs or greater demands. The general effect is to increase the unit costs – that is, the average cost of dealing with each person. Commercial firms, and even mutuals, have the option of adverse selection, or 'cream skimming' (▶ II.3.b.i); governments do not.

An idealized production function for a firm or service is shown in Figure 5. Efficient production is production at the lowest possible unit cost. Initially, when the numbers of people dealt with are few, costs are high. Average costs fall to a point, but after that point they begin to rise as production peaks. The point at which production is most efficient is the bottom of the curve, where the cost per unit is at its lowest. Private sector production is cost-sensitive, and in general a private firm would maximize its returns by minimizing unit costs. That is why the ideal 'free market' produces goods efficiently. But state production cannot be driven primarily by costs; it has to deal with people on the rising part of the

340 M. Keen (1991) *Needs and targeting*, London: Institute for Fiscal Studies.

341 J. Schumpeter (1967) 'Two concepts of democracy', in A. Quinton (ed.) *Political philosophy*, Oxford: Oxford University Press.

342 D. Weimer and A. Vining (1989) *Policy analysis: concepts and practice*, Englewood Cliffs, NJ: Prentice-Hall, ch. 6.

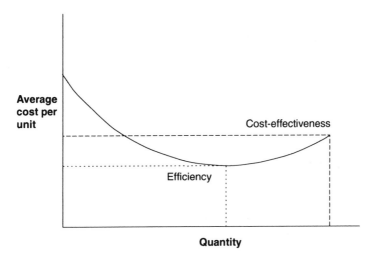

Figure 5   *Efficiency and effectiveness*

curve, even if it is not efficient to do so. The general aim of a social service provided by the state cannot be efficiency; it must be cost-effectiveness – achieving service objectives at the lowest average cost. State production is efficient if, and only if, service objectives happen to coincide with the quantity required for efficiency. This is hardly likely to happen unless efficiency is elevated above other objectives. Provision by the state is inefficient, because the purpose of state provision is to do something else.

III.4.b.iv   *There are other reasons for provision by the state.*

There are several reasons, apart from the delivery of social protection, why states have become involved in welfare provision. One is the adoption of universal standards. The basic argument for universality is an argument for consistency: that people should not be treated differently unless there are relevant differences between them. Minimum standards may be considered requisite for individual rights, freedom or social justice: an example is the introduction of universal elementary education for children.

Another reason for intervention is social control. Allowing independent agencies the use of compulsion can be problematic. Control may be appropriate where one person has to be controlled to protect the rights of another, which is the case in the protection of children from abuse; because the person for whom provision is being made is subject to control, as in the care of prisoners; or as a means of promoting autonomy, which is a central element of arguments for the compulsory detention of mental patients and for compulsory education.

Third, governments have found economic benefits in their engagement in welfare provision. There may be economies of scale. The UK National

Health Service has proved to be substantially more economical than many liberal systems;[343] Italy's introduction of a national system was prompted in part by the desire to achieve similar economies, though subsequently its effectiveness has been challenged from the ideological right.[344]

The production of welfare

III.4.c   The welfare states have come to set the terms on which social protection is delivered.

Governments have a wide range of methods to choose from, which include many measures short of direct coercion. The exercise of direct control by the state is unusual, if only because it requires a level of knowledge and commitment of resources which is beyond the capacity of most agencies. The process of planning can, of course, be based on the kinds of measures already considered – regulation, subsidy, provision, coercion and incentive – among others. For the most part, though, planning is based not on the application of coercive power, but on a process of negotiation and bargaining about outcomes – seeing what can be done, and by what means.

Ironically, this can be difficult in practice to distinguish from the state control of welfare provision. If the outcomes of the welfare system are the outcomes chosen by the state, it comes to the same thing in practice. The important difference is a difference both of method and of principle. The welfare states govern welfare provision; but they did not impose it, and they do not necessarily provide it.

III.4.c.i   Welfare is delivered through many channels.

Welfare is provided in many ways. Conventionally, the distinction is usually made between welfare provided by the state or the public sector, the private sector, voluntary organizations and informal care; but this can be extended at some length.

There is a wide range of public sector policies: Titmuss distinguished social welfare, the provision of social services, from fiscal welfare, which is welfare through the tax system.[345] There are other channels through which welfare can be distributed: the state can make provision as an

---

343 OECD (1990) *Health care systems in transition*, Paris: OECD.

344 M. Niero (1996) 'Italy: right turn for the welfare state?', in V. George and P. Taylor-Gooby (eds) *European welfare policy: squaring the welfare circle*, London: Macmillan; E. Granaglia (1997) The Italian National Health Service and the challenge of privatization, in B Palier (ed.) *Comparing social welfare systems in Southern Europe*, MIRE.

345 R. Titmuss (1963) *Essays on the welfare state*, London: Allen and Unwin.

employer (and in a developed welfare state, government is liable to be one of the largest employers in an economy); the tax system can be used as a means of redistribution or subsidy; the legal system also redistributes resources and makes provision, generally on a compensatory basis. Mutual aid can be distinguished from commercial activity on one hand, and voluntary activity on the other.

The complexity of the system is added to by the high degree of cross-fertilization between the different channels. Public finance can be used for private or voluntary provision, voluntary finance can be used for public provision, and so forth. This has been represented as a 'mixed economy' of welfare.[346] There are different forms of public, corporate, commercial, charitable, and mutualist finance, while provision can be made through the state, the voluntary sector, mutual aid and informal care. Most of the combinations which are possible have been tried at one time or another.

III.4.c.ii   *The welfare states build on other forms of social protection.*

Social protection has grown from a range of sources. The processes which are developed through collective action do not address every area of concern (▶ II.3.b.i); residual elements have to be tackled by government (▶ III.2.c.ii); and there is consequent pressure on governments to expand the range of their activity (▶ III.2.c.iii). This helps to explain one of the central issues in understanding the development of welfare: the emphasis given in different accounts to state or society. If the argument outlined here is correct, both are likely to be true. It is possible to construct accounts of the process which emphasize the scope of collective action at the same time as others which emphasize the role of the state. However, the balance between different forms of action varies, and depends on the circumstances of each society.

In many countries governments came to address the issues of social protection only when collective social services were already partly, or even wholly, formed. The choice these governments faced was either to build on what existed, by accepting and supplementing its provision; to take the existing provision over; or to replace it with their own mechanism.[347] France and the Netherlands, in different ways, generally opted for the first approach; the UK took the second, at least for health services; the former communist states opted for the third. The third option

---

346 K. Judge and M. Knapp (1985) 'Efficiency in the production of welfare: the public and private sectors compared', in R. Klein and M. O'Higgins (eds) *The future of welfare*, Oxford: Blackwell.

347 S. Davies (1997) 'Two conceptions of welfare: voluntarism and incorporationism', in E. Paul, F. Miller and J. Paul (eds) *The welfare state*, Cambridge: Cambridge University Press.

is arguably more common than this suggests; social security in Britain largely took over from the existing friendly societies, despite Beveridge's explicit attempts to protect their position.[348] Ashford, while recognizing the importance of independent organizations within the political process, describes welfare states as 'submerging' independent action.[349] Democratic governments have a tendency to think of themselves as being in charge, whether or not this is the formal arrangement, because they are legitimately in authority and independent or voluntary agencies are not; it is one of the vices which goes with democratic elections.

This seems to imply that the welfare states might drive out independent provision. Perhaps surprisingly, this has proved not to be the case. Rein and van Gunsteren, reviewing pension arrangements, found that just as there was no case in which a shift to private and independent sources could eliminate state provision, there was no case in which state provision had taken over completely from independent sources.[350] The reason for the first part of this finding is clear enough: it stems from the inability of markets to cover the population, and the role of the state as a provider of last resort. The reason for the second part is more perplexing, because it does not have to be true; it seems primarily to testify to the strength of these other arrangements as a basis for social protection.

III.4.c.iii   The action of the state must be seen in the context of existing provision.

The purpose of policy is not necessarily to produce a particular effect – it may be, for example, to institute procedures, or to establish moral principles. However, welfare is concerned with outcomes, and social policy is likely to be designed for welfare. The outcomes of any measure are produced not by the action of the state alone, but by the conjunction of state activity with the effect of other forms of personal and collective action. The value of benefits is the value of the total package received, less any costs which are applied. This is easiest to apply to financial benefits, but it equally applies to other kinds of care package: for example the value of a 'social bath', provided at home by state services, can only be part of a range of services designed to maintain independence in one's own home.[351] Services which are provided in isolation may be seriously ineffective: people discharged from institutions are

---

348 H.E. Raynes (1960) *Social security in Britain*, London: Pitman; W. Beveridge (1942) *Social insurance and allied services*, Cmnd 6404, London: HMSO.

349 D. Ashford (1986) *The emergence of the welfare states*, Oxford: Blackwell, ch. 3.

350 H.V. Gunsteren and M. Rein (1984) 'The dialectic of public and private pensions', *Journal of Social Policy*, 14 (2): 129–150.

351 J. Twigg (1997) 'Deconstructing the "social bath": help with bathing at home for older and disabled people', *Journal of Social Policy*, 26 (2): 211–232.

sometimes rehoused in isolated accommodation with no basic services or support, and the arrangement rapidly collapses. Conversely, there is a risk that services will over-provide, because some other form of provision has already been made: the best example I can think of from my research work is that of an old lady with dementia who was having two breakfasts delivered. Effective help is help which produces desired outcomes, and it is only possible to produce desired outcomes consistently if one knows what the outcome will be.

III.4.c.iv   *The promotion of welfare requires the interweaving of state provision with other forms of solidaristic support.*

The view this prompts of the policy-making process is not one in which the welfare state determines all the production of welfare. What happens, rather, is that policy-makers determine outcomes, assess what is needed to achieve those outcomes, and consider alternative methods by which this can be done.

In a seminal book, Michael Bayley argued that the contribution made by the welfare state itself to the issue he was considering – the care of mentally handicapped people in the community – was marginal, relative to the enormous demands made of families and informal carers. Bayley argued for the 'interweaving' of state and other provision; the state could act most effectively by considering the difference it would make.[352] This concept was at the root of many changes in welfare provision in the 1980s and 1990s, most particularly the policy of 'community care'.

Welfare strategies

III.4.d   The approach to policy affects its nature.

It is possible to treat social policy as a 'black box'. The black box is a scientific method, in which process is ignored; all that is considered is what goes in and what comes out. This technique has made it possible to compare very different systems, particularly in the field of social security: the Luxembourg Income Study compares the total impact of income packages in different countries on distribution, ignoring benefit rules and concentrating instead on their effects.[353]

The main alternative to this approach is expressed by Esping-Andersen, who argues that the methods and processes which are used

---

352 M. Bayley (1973) *Mental handicap and community care*, London: Routledge and Kegan Paul.

353 T.M. Smeeding, M. O'Higgins and L. Rainwater (eds) (1990) *Poverty, inequality and income distribution in comparative perspective*, New York: Harvester Wheatsheaf.

to distribute benefits are an important element of social protection systems.[354] Methods and processes determine the character of the system; quite apart from their distributive impact, there is a profound difference in the experience of benefit receipt in residual and insurance-based systems. They also affect the policy itself, both because they condition the kinds of issues which subsequently arise, and because methods are assumed to define objectives. Empirically, as Esping-Andersen notes, there is a strong connection between residual systems and a limited commitment to welfare expenditure. (The connection is not general, and the reasons for it are in any case disputed. Many commentators argue that residual systems are poor systems, and that the effect of residual welfare is to create stigmatizing divisions which make welfare provision unacceptable.[355] Andries has argued, by contrast, that residual benefits are politically the most firmly founded, and the reason why less money is spent on them is that politicians who want to spend less money are still forced to accept the rationale for residual benefits even if they reject other forms of social protection.)[356]

III.4.d.i Outcomes can be realized in many ways.

Although social policy is not necessarily directed to any end, the commitment to develop welfare tends to imply that certain ends should be pursued, and are likely to be. But there are many different ways to develop welfare, as there would be for any other kind of objective. This broad pattern of policy can be seen as a 'welfare strategy'. A welfare strategy is a set of interrelated policies, adopted on the basis of a common aim or set of approaches. The most common welfare strategies concern broad issues like economic development, redistribution, social protection and the development of solidarity. These issues, which can be pursued singly or in combination, can be tackled in several ways. Particular measures – strategic interventions – can be seen as part of a general strategy, as a contribution to it, and even as a way to deal with the whole issue. It may seem naive to rely on a single method of intervention for a comprehensive strategy – it is more typical for governments in developed countries to introduce a package of measures – but there are examples, such as economic development under Stalin.[357] (Whether it works is another issue.) More commonly, where a particular method is selected, it is believed to be a key to other issues. In economics

---

354 G. Esping-Andersen (1990) *The three worlds of welfare capitalism*, Cambridge: Polity.

355 R.M. Titmuss (1974) *Social Policy: an introduction*, London: Allen and Unwin; P. Townsend (1976) *Sociology and social policy*, Harmondsworth: Penguin.

356 M. Andries (1996) 'The politics of targeting: the Belgian case', *Journal of European Social Policy*, 6 (3): 209–223.

357 A. Nove (1964) *Was Stalin really necessary?* London: Allen and Unwin.

this is widely practised, through the use of single instruments like the interest rate or the exchange rate. The approach has been influential in social work through systems theory, where change can be brought about by key intervention within a specific sub-system.[358]

Strategic intervention is multi-dimensional. The values which inform policy constitute one dimension; the focus of policy (the intended recipient group) is another dimension; the means by which policy is pursued (such as regulation, provision and subsidy) is another. Policy formation, finance, service delivery and the role of users all have claims to be considered as dimensions in their own right. The range of permutations is large, and the outcomes are complex. Interventions, which can themselves be very diverse, are not certain to be internally consistent, let alone consistent with each other.

III.4.d.ii   Methods and processes influence outcomes.

The methods and processes by which social policies are implemented – issues like administration, finance, and service delivery – clearly do matter. From the perspective of the policy-maker, they intervene between the formation of policy and the production of results: they can be seen as a form of inefficiency, diluting the application of effort, but equally they can acquire a life of their own, forcing services down routes which the policy-makers never intended. Lipsky points to the importance of 'street-level bureaucrats', who make decisions at the lowest levels of agencies. These decisions become, effectively, the policy and practice of that agency.[359] From the perspective of the recipient of services, these practices become part and parcel of the service itself; the administrative process, accessibility, the experience of rationing and the say which the user has in the outcomes cannot be distinguished from the policy.

III.4.d.iii   The choice of methods cannot fully be distinguished from the purposes of policy.

By the same argument, the method which is adopted has to be considered as part of the policy. Theoretically and practically, it is quite possible to achieve objectives by ignoring process, concentrating instead on final outcomes, but this is potentially very inefficient, because inputs may not yield proportionate outputs.

Outcomes are directly affected by process. Inequalities in the receipt of health care, for example, are attributable to a range of procedural factors, including (amongst many others) perceptions of need, perceptions of provision, access to health care, the location of service provision, and the

---

358 B. Compton and B. Galaway (1973) *Social work processes*, Homewood, IL: Dorsey; M. Payne (1991) *Modern social work theory*, London: Macmillan.

359 M. Lipsky (1980) *Street level bureaucracy*, London: Sage.

quality of service delivered.[360] Racial disadvantage in public housing has been attributed to the initial status of minority ethnic groups, the effect of adverse policy decisions, access to the housing list, assumptions made about family size and needs, the operation of allocations schemes, and discrimination by officials.[361] These factors are cumulative – none of them substantially explains the problems in itself – and mutually reinforcing. Only a detailed analysis of procedural issues can show how and why policy fails to produce the desired outcomes.

Assessing social policy

III.4.e   Welfare strategies can be assessed by common criteria.

Despite the differences in the welfare states, and differences in strategy, the argument of this book points to a set of evaluative criteria which can be applied to any welfare strategy. Four main areas have been identified in which the operation of the welfare state can be assessed. They are:

(a) *The impact of policy on material welfare, including the relief of poverty and material security.* The welfare state is not focused exclusively on issues of poverty; if anything, its obligations to those who are poor may be weaker than obligations to others (▸ II.1.c.ii). It is, however, concerned with welfare (▸ III.2.a) and with social protection (▸ II.3.a.ii), which means that issues of need, poverty and material security are central to its functions.

(b) *The relationship of the welfare state to the economy, and economic development.* Economic development is a precondition for welfare (▸ II.2.a) and governments have to promote it (▸ III.2.b.i). At least one of the leading models of the welfare state depends on its relationship to the economy (▸ III.2.d.ii).

(c) *The influence of social policy on social relationships, including social cohesion and exclusion.* Social protection has been founded in concerns with security (▸ II.2.b.iii) and solidarity (▸ II.3.a.ii). Social policies may be focused on the problems of exclusion, which are otherwise liable to deny welfare (▸ II.1.b.ii). At the same time, there is some ambiguity surrounding issues of social cohesion (▸ III.2.b.iii), and some of the debates about the legitimacy of government action centre on the potentially negative effects of policies for welfare on social relationships (▸ III.3.c.i).

---

360 P. Townsend, N. Davidson and M. Whitehead (1988) *Inequalities in health*, Harmondsworth: Penguin.

361 D. Smith and A. Whalley (1975) *Racial minorities and public housing*, London: Political and Economic Planning; J. Henderson and V. Karn (1984) *Race, class and state housing*, Aldershot: Gower; Commission for Racial Equality (1989) *Racial discrimination in Liverpool City Council*, London: CRE.

(d) *The effects of the welfare state on social justice, including economic and social inequality.* Issues of inequality have a direct bearing on welfare (▶ II.4.c). The concept of justice is restricted in its scope (▶ II.4.e.i), but within a particular society it has important implications for the distribution of resources (▶ II.4.b) and so for the impact of social policy; governments have a responsibility for the distributive consequences of their actions (▶ III.2.c.iv).

These criteria encompass issues both of method and of outcomes, judged not just by the effects of state intervention but by overall outcomes in the social system.

SUMMARY OF THE ARGUMENT

I   PEOPLE AND SOCIETY

I   People live in society, and have obligations to each other.

I.1   The Person

I.2   Society

I.3   Solidarity

I.4   The Moral Community

II   WELFARE

II   Welfare is obtained and maintained through social action.

II.1   The Nature of Welfare

II.4   Welfare and Redistribution

III   THE STATE AND WELFARE

III   The welfare state is a means of promoting and maintaining welfare in society.

III.1   The Role of the State

III.2   The Welfare States

III.3   Social Policy

III.4   State Action

AFTERWORD

The idea of developing a general theory was drawn from two other books. One is Keynes's *General theory of employment, interest and money*.[362] The other is Hans Kelsen's *General theory of law and state*,[363] which I read many years ago at college. I was not very impressed with Kelsen's work at the time, and I did not refer back to it until after I had largely finished the first draft, but in retrospect I can see some resemblances. My book is, I hope, easier to read, and anyway it has better jokes.

I can identify two main theoretical influences on the book. One has been learning about social policy in France, where many of the ideas in this book – including solidarity, exclusion and the concept of the social network – are commonplace. The second has been the work of Bill Jordan, who has made a series of attempts to root welfare systems in an understanding of social processes rather than political action. He argues that society is based as much in collaboration as in conflict, and that welfare systems emerged through the resolution of these contradictory processes.[364] I discussed some of these points with him at a formal debate some years ago at a Social Administration Association conference. Although I was sympathetic to his emphasis on reciprocity and co-operation, and I think I have shifted further in that direction in the intervening time, I was concerned that he seemed to base social obligation and action solely at the individual level. My attempt to reconcile our positions is, in many ways, fundamental to the argument of this book.

The book's structure was initially intended to follow the pattern of Wittgenstein's *Tractatus logico-philosophicus*.[365] I found it too difficult to

---

362 J.M. Keynes (1936) *The general theory of employment, interest and money*, London: Macmillan.

363 H. Kelsen (1945) *The general theory of law and state*, Cambridge, MA: Harvard University Press.

364 B. Jordan (1987) *Rethinking welfare*, Oxford: Blackwell.

365 L. Wittgenstein (1922) *Tractatus logico-philosophicus*, London: Routledge and Kegan Paul, 1961.

express everything I wanted to say in this format, partly because I was dealing with interrelated phenomena which had no clear lexical ordering, and partly because I was concerned to ground the theory in practical examples. For discussion and illustration, then, I reverted to a more general discussion of those propositions. The result is, I think, quite distinctive; I am sure there must be a book out there which has the same structure, but I do not know what it is.

There are three main tests for theoretical writing. The first is clarity. I have tried to choose language which is simple and direct. This is difficult to do, and I may not have been successful all the way through the book. The ideas I am dealing with are not simple; but if I have done the job properly, they will at least be comprehensible. Of course, this approach has its disadvantages: people who can understand an argument can probably see more easily what is wrong with it. Far too many readers in social science assume that arguments which are impenetrable must be profound; they are much more likely to be badly written.

The second test is organization. This book develops a framework for understanding the welfare state. It is a general theory; I have not tried to cover every important issue in discussions of the welfare state. Many of the subjects are treated very briefly, when they could have been dealt with at much greater length (and have been in my other writing). This is dictated by the structure of the argument. Extended discussion of specific points runs the risk of distorting perspective, or breaking the chain of the argument.

The third test is the strength of the argument. I have tried to strengthen the argument mainly by emphasizing the relationship between its parts, and that is unconventional. I have not undertaken a review of other people's work, for reasons I explained at the outset; if I had, this would have been a very different kind of book. However, I have written a fair amount of work of this kind in the past. *Principles of social welfare* considers a range of normative concepts, including issues like rights, justice, freedom and democracy.[366] *Social policy in a changing society*, written with Maurice Mullard, considers ideological positions, including Marxism, liberalism, conservatism and socialism, as well as a range of views about the way society is changing, including postmodernity, globalization and critical theory.[367] Anyone who wants to consider these other issues can look at these books instead.

Much of my career as a writer has been spent pummelling elderly theories into submission. There comes a point where a reader is entitled to ask, 'But what would you put in their place?' This book is an answer to that question. It is not genuinely original: I have been writing, teaching and researching in social policy for nearly twenty years, and it draws

366 P. Spicker (1988) *Principles of social welfare*, London: Routledge.
367 M. Mullard and P. Spicker (1998) *Social policy in a changing society*, London: Routledge.

heavily on the work I have previously done. Nevertheless, I think I can safely say that this book is not like any other book in social policy.

I have several people to thank for comments on drafts of the book. Hartley Dean, John Veit-Wilson, Brian Smith, Lin Ka, Martin Hewitt, Joanna Poyago-Theotoky, John Dixon and Dominique Spicker have commented on various drafts. There are so many pitfalls in this kind of enterprise that it is unlikely we will have spotted them all, but the book has been greatly improved by their criticisms.

INDEX